Our Exodus Story

Our Exodus Story

Reclaiming the Image of God

Robert P. Vande Kappelle

WIPF & STOCK · Eugene, Oregon

OUR EXODUS STORY
Reclaiming the Image of God

Wipf & Stock
An Imprint of Wipf and Stock Publishers
199 W. 8th Ave., Suite 3
Eugene, OR 97401

www.wipfandstock.com

PAPERBACK ISBN: 978-1-6667-8279-0
HARDCOVER ISBN: 978-1-6667-8280-6
EBOOK ISBN: 978-1-6667-8281-3

06/27/23

Contents

Preface

Books are written and read for a variety of reasons, including to understand and expand meaning, to acquire skills or achieve personal knowledge, and to develop one's potential, but whatever their secondary purpose, their primary purpose is to inform and entertain. Reading books is an essential part of literacy, yet as a leisure activity, such reading is being supplanted by video watching, gaming, and by electronic media. In the United States, where literacy is high, only 5 percent of adults read prolifically—that is, read more than fifty books per year—while only half of adults read one or more books each year for pleasure.

What happens when we stop reading? The short answer is, nothing happens, for if we stop reading, we stay the same. Reading challenges our minds and sparks our curiosity, so if we want to grow in body, mind, and spirit, if we wish to expand our understanding of ourselves and of others, and if we want to live with greater meaning, understanding, and creativity, we must never stop reading.

As author of forty published books and numerous scholarly essays in books and journals, I, too, read for information and entertainment, but also to become a better writer. Like journalists, clergy, and public speakers, authors are constantly looking for new and intriguing topics. This book, like many others in my literary repertoire, deals with the interface of personality and spirituality. In this case, we examine the issue through the lives of four individuals, mirror twins Georgia and Helen and their spouses Jim and Bob. Using a device known as the Myers-Briggs Type Indicator (MBTI), each of these protagonists exhibits distinct dominant personality characteristics, their experiences bearing archetypal relevance and universal appeal. Of our mirror twins, Georgia and Helen, one types as an Intuitive (N), the other as a Feeler (F); and one spouse types as a Sensor

(S), while the other as a Thinker (T).[1] How different individuals can exhibit uniquely diverse dominant personality categories and yet work together, sharing partnership commitment while maintaining individual wholeness, integrity, and joy, is the story of their lives, uniquely and jointly expressed in the following chapters.

The Author's Connection with Georgia and Helen Brown

In 1980, when I began teaching religious studies at Washington & Jefferson College (W&J), a coeducational liberal arts college in Washington, Pennsylvania, some thirty miles south of Pittsburgh, twin sisters Georgia and Helen Brown enrolled in several of my classes—Georgia in a semester-long course on world religions and Helen in a semester-long class on Christianity and then in a January-term course on Christianity-based sectarian movements (then called "cults"). Since these sisters were not enrolled in the same course, I did not know them as twins.

In the fall of 2016, some thirty-six years later and soon after my retirement from full-time teaching, I met Georgia at a college homecoming luncheon. Having recently written commentaries on books of the Bible such as Revelation, the gospel of John, and Old Testament (Hebrew) wisdom literature, I had remained at the college as an adjunct professor teaching this material to students. When I met Georgia, I had recently published an overview of literary, historical and interpretative biblical themes entitled *Securing Life*, and I was eager to promote this book to alumni.

Having gone through the lunch line, I circulated among the tables under the large reception tent, looking for familiar faces, when I spotted Jess Costa, a former student and then a prominent lawyer in southwestern Pennsylvania. He was sitting next to Georgia and her husband Jim Metsger. As I joined them and got reacquainted, Jess and I spoke of our individual journeys to date and Georgia and Jim spoke of their joint journey as a couple. Following lunch, when most alums proceeded to the stadium for the annual homecoming football game, my companions and I strolled to my office, where Georgia and Jim, indicating an interest in *Securing Life*, purchased a copy. Little did we know then that our impromptu gathering would lead to a shared journey together. In the spring of 2017, Georgia and Jim convened a group to study *Securing Life*, and that experience led

1. The Myers-Briggs types and dominant functions are defined and discussed in chapter 2.

to the formation of Body in Spirit, an ecumenical and multicultural group that meets regularly to read and discuss my books and is committed to a panentheistic theology, a unitive anthropological consciousness, and a way of living and thinking called second half of life spirituality. Having written about this perspective, an outlook summarized in a two-volume set of devotional readings entitled *Heart to Heart: The Journey Inward* and *The Journey Outward*, I have been inspired to write the story of Georgia and Helen Brown, now known by their married names Georgia Lee Metsger and Helen Maurine Benson, and their respective spouses, Jim and Bob.

Our Exodus Stories

Central to the biblical narrative is the story of the Exodus, a prototypical account of the journey of faith. The base story is well known. Found in the second book of the Bible, Exodus narrates how Moses helped lead the people of Israel from slavery in Egypt to freedom in the Promised Land. The story includes numerous trials, errors, and failures, including a tumultuous forty-year trek through the wilderness. And when the Israelites cross the Jordan River and enter the land of Canaan, the journey is not over, for life in Canaan would require ongoing risk-taking, punctuated by further trials, errors, failures, and additional exodus stories.

Each of us has an exodus story. In our case, however, the journey is multilayered. On the one hand, it is a biological journey from birth to death, and a social journey from infancy to adulthood. In this regard, it is a story of growing up, of leaving home and taking risks, of making mistakes and learning from them, of reaching goals and surpassing them. As normally conceived, the narrative of life has three phases called past, present, and future.

Spiritually conceived, our exodus stories are journeys into liminal space. Based on the Latin word *limen*, meaning "threshold," liminal space is an inner state and sometimes an outer situation that prompts us to think and act in new ways. Liminality occurs when we are in transition, having left one room or stage in life but not yet entered the next. We usually enter liminal space when our former way of being is challenged or changed—perhaps when we fail at love, are disappointed with others or ourselves, during illness or tragedy, or at major relocations or times of crisis. Liminal space is graced time, but often does not feel "graced" in any way. In such space, we are not certain or in control.

The vulnerability and openness of liminal space allows room for something genuinely new to happen. When we are empty and receptive, we are most teachable, often because we are most humbled. Liminality keeps us struggling with the hidden side of things, calling so-called normalcy into question. It is no surprise that we generally avoid liminal space.

Much of the work of authentic spirituality and human development is to get people into liminal space and to keep them there long enough that they can learn something essential and new. When Christ enters our lives, he isn't showing up to see our perfect schemes. Instead, he invites us into a real, deep, transformative conversation, there at the threshold between who we are and who we can become, if we are willing to let go of what holds us back.

Overview

As collector and editor of the stories in this book, my role involved suggesting, prodding, encouraging, and otherwise teasing out the inspiring narrative as it unfolded. Chapter 1 speaks of human life as a gossamer bridge that binds us as people with God, others, and with our inner being. This journey of faith is described as a "holy balancing act" between the three sources of authority for people of faith—experience, scripture, and tradition. Bonded umbilically to one another and to God, each of us bears Exodus-like and cross-like experiences. Chapter 2 provides an overview of personality and spirituality types, utilizing the psychological theories of Swiss psychiatrist Carl Jung, the spiritual typology developed by Peter Tufts Richardson and Urban Holmes, and the findings of professor of psychology Richard Coan regarding the nature of the optimal human personality.

Chapter 3 introduces the ancestral history of mirror twins Georgia Lee Metsger and Helen Brown Benson, followed by six chapters narrating the individual and combined stories of Georgia and Helen and their respective spouses, Jim and Bob. The closing chapter introduces core social motives that help readers broaden the base for comprehending not only the life stories of our four protagonists but also their own Exodus journeys.

As people progress in life, they discover that maturity involves overcoming adversity, becoming aware of individual strengths and weaknesses, admitting wrongdoing, forgiving themselves and others, embracing who they have become, and remaining hopeful of their future. When it comes to self-awareness, three factors seem prominent: (1) awareness of one's thoughts, desires, and actions; (2) assuming responsibility for one's thoughts, desires, and actions; and (3) knowing why one thinks, desires, or acts as one does, that is, having awareness of what drives one's personality, needs, wants, desires, and actions. In this regard, some knowledge of personality theory is useful, for in addition to helping us understand ourselves, such knowledge helps us better understand our mates, family members, relatives, friends, coworkers, teammates, neighbors, rivals, and adversaries.

I write this book from my perspective as an ordained Presbyterian minister and a career professor of religious studies. In addition, I am credentialed to administer and interpret the Myers-Briggs Type Indicator (MBTI) by The Association for Psychological Type, which enables me to administer and teach psychological and spiritual testing and typing to students and adults in college, community, and church settings.

The stories in this book, individual and combined, are epic, the protagonists and families as complex as their biblical patriarchal and matriarchal counterparts, yet as current as today's top stories. As you read, you will be invited on your own inner journey to peace, wholeness, and well-being. It is hoped that the result of such journeys, whether for ourselves or our family, friends, and communities, will bring healing and hope to many in these divisive and troubling times.

1

The Gossamer Bridge

One of the central teachings of Christian anthropology is that humans are made in the "image of God." In the first chapter of Genesis we read these words: "Let us make humankind in our image, according to our likeness; and let them have dominion over . . . the earth" (Gen 1:26). While it is not clear what it means to say that humans are made in the "image" of God—that idea is never systematically explained in the Bible—it cannot refer to physical likeness, for the writer of Genesis 1 takes pains to stress the holiness and transcendence of God. Nevertheless, that concept clearly is central to what it means to be human. Concerning the phrase "image of God" (often referred to by the Latin phrase *Imago Dei*), the following meanings apply:

- Humankind's nature. Because humans are created in the image of God, they have a moral and spiritual nature. Having a God-given freedom provides both dignity and responsibility. As image bearers, they see situations, persons, and things nondualistically, that is, from the perspective of oneness, a way of seeing that is "both/and" rather than exclusively "either/or."
- Humankind's position. Being made in the image of God implies personhood and attributes to human beings a unique relationship with God. As persons, humans are related to God in a manner different from anything else in the created order.
- Humankind's function. Since human beings are uniquely related to God by creation, the Old Testament states that their primary function

is to worship and serve the Creator in every aspect of life. Furthermore, as God's vice-regents, they are given ecological responsibility over nature.

- Humankind's capability. As image bearers, human beings are endowed with creativity. As co-creators with God, their way of living, thinking, and being is spiritual, a pilgrimage home. When they are creative, they are living out of the resources of their True Self.
- The universality of the image. Genesis 1:27 tells us that both male and female are created in God's image. In the creation account, Adam and Eve represent all humanity. Indeed, the word "Adam" is not a proper name in Hebrew, but merely a word meaning "humankind." Likewise, the word "Eve" is the Hebrew word for "life" or "living." The *Imago Dei* is not the sole possession of one tribe or race or nation. Its potential applies to every human being without exception.

According to this understanding, while we humans are *in* nature, we stand *above* nature, for we have the freedom to acknowledge the claims of the Creator upon us and, within that relationship, to exercise dominion over the earth. Because we stand in a personal relation with God, we humans are the crowning glory of God's creation (Ps 8:5–8).

What does it mean to be human? we ask. What makes a person unique? Does biology have priority? Are personality and spirituality equally significant factors? What about race, gender, and social class? To what extent are we shaped by our upbringing or education, by our friends and loved ones? What roles do our jobs and accomplishments play in our self-image and identity?

When our Western forebears thought of personhood, they searched the realm of art and drama for guidance, settling on the term "person" as definitive. The word "person" comes from the Latin word for "mask" or for the actor's role in a drama. The Judeo-Christian tradition builds on this idea, viewing human personhood as an organic participation in the one personhood that is God. In other words, the human self has no meaning or substance apart from the Selfhood of God. God's personhood, however, is not a mask, but the face behind all masks. We humans are the masks of God, and we play out God's image in myriad ways.

As icons of God, human beings are endowed with the unique capacity to mirror and reflect the character of God. While the divine character cannot be defined exhaustively or comprehensively, its nature—holy, just, and eternal—is clearly loving, compassionate, forgiving, and altogether creative.

The Two Selves

The ultimate adventure, the grandest game, the greatest challenge, is the spiritual transformation of the self. As I discuss in my 2019 book, *Walking on Water*, the role of authentic spirituality is letting go of the false self, one's incomplete self trying to pass for one's True Self. Our True Self, our inherent soul, is that part of us that sees reality accurately, truthfully. It is divine breath passing through us, dwelling with us. Our false self is the egoic self that is limited and constantly changing. It masquerades as true and permanent but in reality is passing, tentative, and fearful of change. It is that part of us that will eventually die. The role of true spirituality, of mature religion, is to help speed up this process of dying to the false self.

Not surprisingly, we cannot accomplish—or even understand—what we have not been told to look for or to expect. This staggering change of perspective—that our ego is not our True Self—is what Jesus came to convey to humanity. It led Thomas Merton, the Trappist monk who first suggested use of the term false self, to his radical rediscovery of the meaning of Jesus' teaching that his followers must lose their false self in order to discover their True Self (see Mark 8:35).

This realization—what some people call "mindfulness" and mystics call "being present"—is the heart of religious transformation (meaning, "to change forms"). For Christians, the model and exemplar of such transformation is Jesus, who came to tell us—and show us—that our human form is also divine, that what is human also shares in the divine nature, a divinely implanted reality that can be experienced here and now, in our present mortal state. Initially, that possibility might sound far-fetched, but I assure you, that concept is both true and truly Christian.

However, according to Christian teaching, that image (our True Self) has been marred, corrupted, and displaced by an ego-driven false self. If that is so, what would it be like to reclaim this image, and hence to recover our original goodness, affirming harmony with God, others, ourselves, and the earth, whose image we also bear? What would it be like to live up to our spiritual potential and according to our divine nature? And what would this be like not only individually but also jointly, in communion with others? As this book suggests, the journey of recovery begins individually, then proceeds jointly with siblings and spouses/partners, modeling this interconnectedness initially with family and friends and then outwardly to communities of work, worship, and play, like a stone cast into water creates ripples that flow outwardly and exponentially.

Spirituality, traditionally defined by Christians as "life in the Spirit," encompasses the journey of life from a distinct perspective. Spirituality is the journey of life "from God, to God, and with God." As a result, it is also a journey toward self. In other words, the process of coming to know or to experience God is also the process of knowing oneself. Through this process, one comes to differentiate between one's temporary or false self, which we call the ego, and one's permanent or True Self, that part of us made in the image of God and made for ongoing or everlasting relationship with God. In the end, we discover that we know God by being known, much like one loves by being loved.

As is becoming evident to many spiritual seekers nowadays, all larger-than-life people we have ever known have one denominator in common: in some sense, they have all died before they died, meaning each was led to the edge of their private resources to experience a sense of deprivation that surely felt like dying. Yet that breakdown, that loss, led them into a larger life. They went through a death of their various false selves and came out on the other side knowing that their death could no longer hurt them. They fell into the Great Love and the Great Freedom—which many call God.

Throughout most of history, the journey through Death into Life was taught in sacred space and ritual form, which clarified, distilled, and shortened the process. Today, many people don't learn how to move past their fear of diminishment, and this absence of training in grief work and letting go, this failure to entrust ourselves to a greater life, has contributed to our culture's spiritual crisis.

True spirituality is about letting go. Instead, we have made it to be about attaining, performing, winning, and succeeding. Authentic spirituality, prompted by the struggles and experiences of our exodus journeys, echoes the paradox of life itself. It trains us in both detachment and attachment: detachment from the transitory so we can attach to the enduring. If we do not acquire good training in detachment, we may attach to the wrong things, especially to our egoic self and its desire for aggrandizement and security. Each time we let go of what we think might bring us personal happiness, we invariably find ourselves in a larger, a larger space, a deeper union, a greater joy. However, this truth cannot be proven theoretically or ahead of time, for it can only be known after the fact. As people in the second half of life can discern by looking back at their lives, little of substance is ever lost by falling, and nothing of value is ever lost by loving. By falling, we find; by letting go, we gain; by losing self we discover. Life is a spiritual journey toward union, a process of falling upward.

The Triangle of Faith

According to bestselling writer David Baldacci, "The passing down of memories is the strongest link in the gossamer bridge that binds us as people; what we hold in our hearts is truly the fiercest component of our humanity.[1]

In our journey homeward, toward our True North, each of us needs a dependable beacon or compass, a reliable base, foundation, or authority. The "triangle of faith" is a wisdom paradigm that guides authentic religion and spirituality. Described as a "holy balancing act" to illustrate the dynamic interrelationship between the three sources of authority for people of faith—experience, scripture, and tradition—the front wheel is experience and the two back wheels are scripture and tradition.

The value of using this metaphor to illustrate the journey of faith is that as a relatively stable three-wheeled vehicle, the tricycle enables passengers to move forward but also backward when necessary. While moving backward is impossible on a two-wheeled bicycle, such movement is possible on a tricycle, although such movement can be awkward and unwieldy. While moving backward is possible on a tricycle, such vehicles are most efficient moving forward. The front wheel, essential to turning and motion, is experience. This might come as a surprise to many traditional believers, particularly Protestants, Catholics, and Orthodox Christians who typically base their belief systems on scripture and/or tradition. However, authentic spirituality, while often derived from scripture or religious tradition, is invariably filtered through personal experience.

Whereas conventional Christians tend to think of tradition as monolithic or unified, in actuality the tradition upon which the church was founded was diverse and varied. For the first five hundred years, Christians were distinguished by Hebraic, Greek, and Roman methodological, epistemological, social, and literary approaches and perspectives. Thereafter, they were divided by orthodox and sectarian Christian traditions, and later by Italian, French, German, and British religious traditions. In

1. Baldacci, *Wish You Well*, 127.

actuality, there never was one Christian Tradition with a capital "T," only traditions with a small "t."

Likewise, when it comes to scripture, while since the fourth century most Christians have adhered to a common canon, at least of the New Testament writings, there is the issue of interpretation. While Christians might be connected by scripture, they have been divided by interpretation, since all reading of scripture is interpretive and necessarily divisive. Because the language of the Bible is largely poetic or metaphorical, readers must decide when to read literally and when metaphorically. And if they rely on religious authorities for meaning, they soon come to realize that such authorities often disagree among themselves on meaning and application.

Awareness of these issues lead to the conclusion that scripture and tradition—the rear wheels of the metaphorical "triangle of faith"—are based on the subjective biases of faith systems. While scripture and tradition are often used to validate one another, together they are dependent on the dynamic third principle of divine guidance, personal experience. Alone, the front wheel of a tricycle is useless, but when held accountable to scripture and tradition and under mature spiritual guidance and counsel, the "tricycle of faith" operates as a fully functioning authority system. While the wheels of scripture and authority can be seen as sources of outer authority, personal experience provides inner authority. People of faith can and must have all three, for when inner and outer authority come together, they comprise true spiritual wisdom. By itself, information from outer authority is not necessarily transformative, and what is needed today are genuinely transformed people, not just people with traditional answers.

The Common Human Bond: Our Umbilical Connection

At birth and during gestation in the womb, every human being is connected to his or her mother by an umbilical cord, and as a reminder of that connected identity, each of us has only to gaze at our belly button. Likewise, each of us is connected umbilically at birth to our divine Mother. While during our lifetime this eternal connectedness is regularly torn, violated, and neglected, it is never fully severed, as evidenced by the Spirit deep within us all, which we call the "image of God." As we nourish, cultivate, and otherwise affirm this spiritual connection, we affirm our umbilical connection with human beings of all time, past, present, and future, for spirituality is eternal. Because we are all connected umbilically with God, it is both natural and true to affirm that we are all umbilically connected to one another. While this connection is often torn, violated, and neglected, it is never severed, as evidenced by the one divine image within us, the common human bond that unites us all. What I am suggesting is that when we look at another person, we see reflected in their spiritual aura our own divine image. As native Americans put it, "Let the God in me see the God in you."

In the New Testament gospels, we hear Jesus inviting people to follow him, to walk with him, to go on a journey. As we learn from Christian history, the history of each believer, as that of the church, is the story of two spiritual journeys—the interior journey toward knowing our True Self and knowing God, and the journey directed outward into the world to enact God's justice and love. These two movements, both Godward, comprise the way of Jesus, a continual flow of breath inward and outward.

This quest is a mapless journey, for there is no single path or route; the only guides to it are the mystics, sages, and saints of all places, who tell their stories through poetry, narrative, and song, relying on the triple witnesses of nature, experience, and Spirit. The medieval Christian mystic Meister Eckart spoke of this journey as one "without destination. There is no map. Your soul will lead you. And you can take nothing with you."[2]

Our Common Human Bond: The Cross as Symbol

If, as Jesuit theologian Richard Rohr emphasizes in *The Universal Christ*, the term "Christ" represents the eternal union of matter and Spirit from the beginning of time, and Jesus represents a unique incarnation of the cosmic Christ, then that Christ must be viewed, not as a solitary figure, but as a universal reality that includes all humanity and all of creation since the beginning of time (see Rom 1:20). Thus, whenever the material and the spiritual coincide, there is the Christ. According to this perspective, Christ (and therefore God) need not be viewed as "out there" or "over there," for God is in us, here, now, and everywhere. Each human is a little word of God, a mini-incarnation of divine love. The goal, however, is not to focus on ourselves but to move beyond ourselves, recognizing that what is true in us is true in others as well. The Universal Christ permeates all creation, for human beings are the image and likeness of God!

While Christians traditionally consider the expression "Jesus Christ" as an exalted name for Jesus of Nazareth, we must remember that the term

2. Davies, Oliver, *Meister Eckhart: Select Writings*, 246–47.

"Christ" (a Greek translation of the Jewish word "messiah," meaning "one anointed or appointed to a sacred office") was introduced by later followers of Jesus as a term that came to mean much more than a name, including a preexistent deity, the incarnate deity, and the second member of the Trinity. However, when we think of the Jesus of history, I suggest we think of the historical human being who represents for Christians the ideal universal person, the embodiment of the highest and best in us all, the one who bears the ideal of normality and universality simultaneously. If Christ represents the resurrected state of human life, then Jesus represents the crucified path of getting there. "If Christ is the source and goal [of human life], then Jesus is the path from the source toward the goal of divine unity with all things."[3]

It is not insignificant that Christians chose the cross as their central symbol, for Christian discipleship ultimately and unavoidably leads to the cross of Jesus, for believers a call to identify with the pain of the world. At least unconsciously, we recognize that Jesus talked often about "losing" our lives. Perhaps Ken Wilber's distinction between "ascending religions" and "descending religions" is helpful here. While traditional Christianity often avoided thinking of the cross as a call to discipleship by softening it or making it into a theory of moral perfection or of divine favoritism that leads to "going to heaven," converting others rather than ourselves, and acquiring better health and greater success and wealth in this world, Wilber trusts descending religion much more, as Jesus certainly did.[4] Here the primary implication is not self-development or individual salvation, for the cross represents a call to service, to incarnation in the pain and suffering of others. Authentic Christianity is not so much a belief system as a life-and-death system that shows us how to give away our life, how to give away our love, and eventually how to give away our death. Essentially, as we give ourselves away, we connect with the world, with all other creatures, and with God.[5]

In the fourth century, when Christianity was embraced by Emperor Constantine and ended up aligning with empires, wars, and colonization of our planet, instead of aligning with Jesus or the powerless, it lost its way. Unlike the way of those who emphasize ascending over descending, authentic Christianity takes us to the cross of Jesus, to solidarity with those on the margins of society. Likewise, authentic spirituality takes us to the cross

3. Rohr, *Universal Christ*, 216.

4. Cited in Rohr, *Universal Christ*, 216.

5. Rohr, *Universal Christ*, 212–13.

of our own humiliations, loss, and shame. Spirituality is about honoring the human journey, loving it and living it in all its wonder and tragedy. There is nothing really "supernatural" about love and suffering. It is completely natural, taking us through the deep interplay of death and life, surrender and forgiveness, in all their configurations.

The cross consists of two crossmembers, one horizontal and the other vertical. As we reach outward and downward, we invariably expand inward and upward. By loving others as extensions of ourselves, we love God. That's the way—the only way—it works. Like the image of God within all human beings, the universal cross of human experience binds us to one another and to our divine Lover and Redeemer. As theologian Cynthia Bourgeault notes, while the account of Jesus' passion has often led to manipulative, guilt-inducing theology, when she reads the events regarding Jesus' betrayal, trial, and execution on the cross, she understands Jesus' life as a sacrament, that is, as a sacred mystery whose primary purpose is not to arouse empathy but to create empowerment. In other words, cross theology is not about increasing our guilt or our devotion, but rather about deepening our personal capacity to make the passage into unitive life.[6]

Our Exodus Story takes us on two journeys, one downward and the other upward. It takes us on the journey of the cross experience of four individuals, and through them, to our own cross experiences. Though bruised by outer and inner processes and circumstances, each protagonist seeks spiritual wholeness in spite of—or perhaps because of or through—trying circumstances. But the narrative does not leave readers lost in sadness and despair. Rather, our common cross experiences become conduits and guides to the further, higher journey of glory and grace, of salvation and restoration, to the joyous reclamation of our heritage as sons and daughters of the eternal God, fully and forever members of the family of God.

The Spiritual Journey

While the journey of life involves growing physically, emotionally, and intellectually, it is essentially spiritual in nature, for it is a journey toward God. This spiritual journey, like the physical journey, also consists of three phases: from autonomy to morality, from ignorance to belief, and from belief to faith. Another model to theological, existential, and spiritual development speaks of precritical, critical, and postcritical phases or stages, where

6. Bourgeault, *Wisdom Jesus*, 104–6.

individuals progress from an early simplicity, where they accept whatever significant authority figures in their lives tell them to be true as indeed true, through the phase of critical understanding, where individuals trust critical reason or doubt over faith and trust, to postcritical or second simplicity, where individuals understand their lives as open-ended journeys in which they seek, not an end to existential ambiguity and uncertainty, but rather breadth, depth, and meaning. While it is both possible and probable for individuals to get stuck in the first or second stages of their journey, those who progress to the third stage or phase realize that life is a pilgrimage, and that the entire earth can become hallowed ground and therefore the locus of encounter with the living God. Such individuals may be said to have enter second half of life living, thinking, and being, also called second half of life spirituality.

This "further journey" is not chronological, nor does one magically stumble upon it at midlife or in times of crisis, though these often serve as catalysts. While the second journey represents the culmination of one's faith journey, it is largely unknown today, even by people we consider deeply religious, since most individuals and institutions remain stymied in the preoccupations of the first half of life, establishing identity, creating boundary markers, and seeking security. The first-half-of-life task, while essential, is not the full journey. Furthermore, one cannot walk the second journey with first-journey tools. One needs a new toolkit.

The first task is to build a strong "container" or identity; the second is to find the contents that the container is meant to hold.[7] The first task—surviving successfully—is obvious, one we take for granted as the purpose of life. We all want to complete successfully the task that life first hands us: establishing an identity, a home, a career, relationships, friends, community, and security, all foundational for getting started in life. Many cultures throughout history, most empires in antiquity, and the majority of individuals in the modern period have focused on first-half-of-life tasks, primarily because it is all they have time for, but also for lack of vision.

Most of us are never told that we can set out from the known and the familiar to take on a further journey. Our institutions, including our churches, are almost entirely configured to encourage, support, reward, and validate the tasks of the first half of life. Shocking and disappointing as it may be, we struggle more to survive than to thrive, focusing on "getting through" or on getting ahead rather than on finding out what is at the top or was already at

7. Rohr, *Falling Upward*, xiii.

the bottom. As wilderness guide Bill Plotkin puts it, many of us learn to do our "survival dance," but we never get to our actual "sacred dance."

In his book *Faith After Doubt*, postmodern Christian theologian Brian McLaren proposes a four-stage model of faith development. He labels the four stages, Simplicity, Complexity, Perplexity, and Harmony. McLaren compares these stages to the four sequential seasons of spring, summer, fall, and winter, likening Simplicity to the springlike season of spiritual awakening, Complexity to the summerlike season of spiritual strengthening, Perplexity to the autumnlike season of spiritual surviving, and Harmony to the winterlike season of spiritual discovery. Each new stage, like a ring on a tree, embraces and builds upon the previous stage, while growing beyond its limits. Alternatively, each stage includes and transcends its predecessors.

Like living with nature, the point is not to stay in spring or summer forever, nor is it the point to get to (or through) winter as soon as possible, any more than the point of life is advancing from infancy to old age as soon as possible. Rather, the point is to live each stage fully, to learn well what each day and season has to teach, and to live and enjoy life in companionship with God and others through all of life's seasons. As with nature, the journey of faith is not a neat progression, and the lines between stages are certainly arbitrary. The fact is, there is no more of a clear line between stages than there is a clear line between seasons. You can have warm days in winter and snowfall in spring, and just as calendars don't tell the whole story, neither can any schema. There is no shame, pride, or regret in being at the stage of development in which we find ourselves. If there is anything to regret, I suppose it is refusing to grow when life invites us to do so, or rushing through our current stage without learning all it has to teach us.

Simplicity, the stage of authority, is the baseline of what being raised means in out culture. Here one is taught the basis of morality, particularly the difference between right and wrong. While this stage works well for children and adolescents, many people spend their entire lives in this phase, submitting to authorities and following all the rules. Then, when it is time for them to become authorities themselves, they demand the same submission from the next generation that they themselves gave to the previous generation. For that reason, it shouldn't be a surprise that faith and religion are a strictly Stage One phenomenon for millions, even billions, of people.

If Stage One is about dualism and dependence, Stage Two is about pragmatism and independence. We have our own lives to live, and we have to find a way to become who we are on our own. In Stage One we were drawn to authority figures who told us what to think and do, but in Stage Two we seek out coaches who teach us how to think for ourselves and help us develop our own goals, along with our own skills to attain those goals. In Stage One, we saw life as a matter of survival, but in Stage Two we see life as a game, as a contest of competing and winning. In Stage One everything was either known or knowable, but in Stage Two, everything is learnable and doable, if only we can find the right models, mentors, and coaches, and master the right techniques, skills, and know-how.

In terms of our faith, we are no longer content merely to listen to a sermon by an authority figure; we want to learn methods of studying the Bible for ourselves. Learning and studying, thinking for ourselves and reaching our own conclusions, are part of what it means to be a good Stage Two Christian. People in Simplicity and Complexity become active consumers in the religious market. Every year, they need more sermons, books, radio and TV shows, podcasts, conferences, courses, retreats, camps, churches, and mission trips. For some people, the only faith they will ever know is either the authoritarian, dualistic faith of Stage One, or the pragmatic independent faith of Stage Two. However, what happens if you start to question your religious goals?

When people run into problems with Stage Two faith, some believers temporarily or permanently revert to Stage One forms of faith. Some, however, start doubting the whole faith project. They begin to feel so stuck, trapped, and stagnant they decide to burn down the whole structure. Other people aren't so easily satisfied. Their quest for honesty and depth burns like a fire in the belly and they move into Stage Three (Perplexity). Life for people in Stage Three feels more than simple and more than complex; it is simultaneously perplexing and mysterious. Because this stage embraces relativism, Stage Three people feel more comfortable lurking on the fringes of a group rather than belonging squarely in its center. Even better, they might be fringe members of a number of groups, to gain a variety of viewpoints. Unable to find a community that fits their stage, many become unaffiliated "nones," working out their questions alone. If they find community at all, it tends to be among alienated individuals like themselves. Now everything they once constructed they now deconstruct. Will anything remain, or will they end up in a state of spiritual bankruptcy?

Over time, many come to see that their grim "all is lost" assessment isn't the whole story. People deep in Perplexity, feeling disillusioned with naïve dualism and pragmatism, face a stark choice. Will they become cynical nihilists, seeing everything so critically that meaning, purpose, value, reverence, and wonder become increasingly distant and elusive? For some people, this cynicism is the only intellectually honest option, so they surrender to perpetual Perplexity, all dressed up in critical thinking with nowhere to go. Nevertheless, some people can't be satisfied with that choice. They become cynical of their own cynicism, skeptical of their own skepticism, critical of their own critical thinking, even doubting their doubtfulness. They begin to wonder, hope, and imagine, and they dare to believe that there is another option beyond Stage Three. To maintain momentum, to keep growing and developing, however, requires a kind of dying, a death to ego or pride, a relinquishment of our right to judge, to know, and to control. You might call this a death to privilege, superiority, or supremacy, as seekers realize that all people share in the human condition.

Stage Four (Harmony) builds on "the still more excellent way of love" described by Paul in his letter to the Corinthians (1 Cor 12:31—14:1). In this passage, Paul makes clear that nearly everything religious people strive for will eventually be embraced by something deeper. Even faith and hope don't have the last word. Only love, he says, is the more excellent way. In his masterpiece *The Brothers Karamazov*, Dostoyevsky captured this shift to Clarity when he admonished his readers to "Love all God's creation, the whole and every grain of sand in it. Love every leaf, every ray of God's light. Love the animals, love the plants, love everything. If you love everything, you will perceive the divine mystery in things. Once you perceive it, you will begin to comprehend it better every day. And you will come at last to love the whole world with an all-embracing love."

At some point, this discovery of unifying Harmony beyond disintegrating Perplexity seems very simple, almost childish, like a return home. Perhaps this is what T. S. Eliot had in mind when he wrote, "We shall not cease from exploring, and the end of our exploring will be to arrive where we started and know the place for the first time." For this reason, Harmony has been described as a second naiveté, a second simplicity or innocence best described as transcendence, a transcendence, however, that combines the best of the conservative and the best of the progressive positions, because it brings along or includes the previous stages rather than leaving them behind.

If in Stage One we know that everything is knowable, in Stage Two we know that everything is doable, and in Stage Three we know that everything is relative, in Stage Four we come to know that everything is suitable for its time (Eccl 3:11). In this stage we can finally accept that all our knowing, past and present, is partial (1 Cor 13:12). Now we finally see authority figures neither as omniscient and trustworthy (as in Stages One and Two) nor as fake or deluded (as in Stage Three), but rather as human beings like us, mortal and fallible. This awareness also allows us to find our identity in new ways in relation to others; not in Stage One dependence, nor in Stage Two independence, and not in Stage Three counterdependence, but in the more mature interdependence of nonduality. This humility before others morphs into what some call paradoxy—the realization that no statement about God—or even about what is true—can be final or complete.

This new realization—likened to a second Simplicity—eventually matures into a higher Complexity, and so on, in an ascending spiral of growth and discovery that continues as long as life itself. Far from feeling we have finally arrived, in Stage Four we finally begin to understand that arrival has never been the goal.

In Stage Four we discover amazing truths. For example, we discover that spirituality is about love; that knowing is loving; that we know ourselves by loving ourselves; that we know others by loving them; that we know God by loving ourselves and others. Those who reach Stage Four do not experience Certainty, however, for that is the concern of those in Stages One and Two. Stage Four people never feel they have arrived. They are not obsessed with misguided notions of certainty or supremacy—more the opposite. Committed to the faith journey, they know there is no such thing as certainty in faith. Faith, like all creativity, flourishes not in certainty but in questioning, not in security but in venturing. In Stage Four, it is trust that matters, and qualities such as peace, harmony, joy, relationships, intimacy, and unity.

Those who reach Stage Four can also look back and see love's gravitational pull all along. When they loved correctness in Stage One, the love with which they pursued correctness mattered more. When they loved effectiveness in Stage Two, the love that moved them to pursue effectiveness mattered still more. When they loved honesty and justice in Stage Three, honesty and love mattered, but the love that burned in their heart for them mattered still more. Faith was about love all along. They just didn't realize it, and it took doubt to help them see it.

While the Bible can be read for theological information, it also provides a narrative in faith formation, for all four stages of faith appear in the biblical storyline. The biblical narrative begins with Torah, that is, with teaching suitable to Stage One formative faith, including stories of beginnings, both of the cosmos and of the Hebrew people as a theocratic community in covenant relationship with God. It then moves into the monarchical or kingdom phase, where the covenant community becomes unified as Israel before dividing into two kingdoms, northern Israel and southern Judah. Over time, both kingdoms come to an end politically, in the exilic and postexilic phases. For Christians, the biblical narrative does not end with postexilic Judaism, but rather moves through the Intertestamental Period to its culmination in Jesus, the apostolic period, and the emergence of the church.[8]

8. For further information on the unfolding drama of faith in the biblical storyline, see Vande Kappelle, *Outgrowing Cultic Christianity*, 155–62.

2

Personality and Spirituality Theory

PEOPLE ARE NATURALLY DIFFERENT from one another in fundamental ways: we want different things, have different aims, think and learn differently, and believe differently. And of course, how we act and emote is governed by individual needs, desires, and beliefs. In many cases, differences in others trigger negative responses in ourselves. Seeing others differing from us, it is easy to conclude that when they differ from us in behavior or response, it is due to some malady or flaw. Our job, at least for those near us, might seem to be to correct their flaws, making those near us more like ourselves. Such a task, however, is doomed from the start. Attempts to change others, whether spouse, sibling, lover, co-worker or friend, can produce change, but the results are likely more distortions than transformations. Besides, trying to change others is futile and counterproductive, in that most of the differences between is are essentially good.

Jungian Personality Theory

The belief that people are fundamentally alike appears to be a twentieth century notion. The idea is probably related to the growth of democracy in the Western world. If we are equals, we must be alike. Classical psychologists such as Freud, Adler, Sullivan, Fromm, and their followers affirmed the idea of singular motivation. Whatever the drive, whether motivated by Eros, power, social solidarity, or the search after Self, each personality school made one instinct primary for everybody.

Swiss psychiatrist Carl Jung (1875–1961) disagreed. He noted that people differ in fundamental ways, even though they all possess the same instincts to drive them from within. No instinct is more important than another; what is most significant for most individuals, however, is their preference for how they function. Because people are characterized by their preference for given functions, they may be "typed" by their preference.

One of the most important contributions of Carl Jung to modern psychological thought is his theory of personality types. While Jung's monumental study, *Psychological Types*, requires a good deal of psychological and philosophical background to be understood, the essentials of his theory have been elaborated and developed by others, including the personality type indicator developed by Isabel Briggs-Myers and her mother Katherine Cook Briggs known as the Myers-Briggs Type Indicator (MBTI), which charts sixteen possible personality types in terms of Jungian type theory. Today, thanks to this sorting device, many Jungian concepts are widely known and accepted and millions have taken the MBTI, which is widely applied in team building, organization development, business management, education, and career and marriage counseling. Understanding one's type is making a welcome change in people's lives globally, in a wide diversity of situations.

If you have never taken the MBTI, or if you need to verify your personality type, I recommend that you take an online version of the test.[1] But before you do, keep in mind that the MBTI is not really a test, but a sorter of preferences on four scales or categories, each consisting of two opposite poles. There is no "right" or "wrong" answer. In order to get accurate results, adopt a relaxed demeanor and remember that you are attempting to discover your preferred answer to each question, not what you or your parents or anyone else wished you preferred as an answer. Since humans are complex individuals, our preferences may vary from situation to situation. The MBTI reports preferences on four scales, each consisting of two opposite poles. The following exercise conveys what Jung and Myers meant by "preferences":

1. Though online resources frequently change, I recommend you try the free test found on 16personalities.com. The personality descriptors for our four protagonists, found in chapters 4, 5, 7, and 8 below are adapted from the personality descriptions found on this website.

First, on the line below sign your name as you normally do;

____

Now, sign your name again on the line below, but this time use your other hand;

____

The first result was effortless and natural, the second awkward and unnatural. Similarly, according to the theory, everyone has a natural preference for one of the two opposites on each of the four MBTI scales. You use both preferences at different times, but not both at once and not, in most cases, with equal confidence.

At the conclusion of the test you receive four letters, which comprise your personality type. They indicate the differences in people that result from

- where they prefer to focus their attention (Extraversion or Introversion)—E or I;
- the way they prefer to take in information (Sensing or Intuition)—S or N;
- the way they prefer to make decisions (Thinking or Feeling)—T or F;
- how they orient themselves to the external world (Judging or Perceiving)—J or P.

These preferences produce sixteen different kinds of people, interested in different things and drawn to different fields. Each type has its own inherent strengths as well as its likely blind spots. However, these types often blend into one another, inasmuch as each of us is a unique combination of these attitudes and functions. Discovering one's personality type is extremely beneficial, for it influences career choices, marriage choices, learning style, spiritual journeys, theological understanding, and much more. Learning one's personality type also makes us more aware and sensitive to the psychological needs, preferences, and differences of those around us.

If we are to care for, work with, or love other people, we need to know what makes them unique, and we will need to help them develop their own type potential and relate to them in ways that are meaningful to them. For example, people with developed sensate functions are usually characterized by simplicity in life style. They are interested in concrete facts and seldom in fantasy or make-believe. The basic interest of the intuitive type is in acquiring wisdom. Unlike sensors, they are fascinated by fantasy, hunches, and imaginative possibilities. However, routine tasks often bore them and they often do not follow through. They need new challenges, new problems, variety, and change. The thinking type wants things understandable and in logical order; consequently, thinkers do not like exceptions to rules. Often they make good executives, because the good of the whole takes precedence over individual desires. They can make decisions, but sometimes their apparent coldness alienates other types. The feeling type is most often characterized by an ability to experience joy. It is important to realize that the word "feeling" does not mean emotion, but rather signifies the capacity to evaluate data according to human values. Feelers are interested in other human beings and what influences them. They are excellent at getting along with others and are often found in the helping professions. Making unpleasant decisions affecting the lives of others is difficult for them.

It is impossible to love others unless we can recognize their type and place an adequate value upon their primary function. But here's a caveat: We should never try to have other persons change their type. They will do best if they develop what they are by nature.

Type Dynamics: Determining Dominance

Of the two middle letters in your type (S or N, T or F), one will be your dominant function, your home base of operations; the other will be your auxiliary, your second most important function. The following formula determines how to locate these functions; it is a bit tricky at first, so study it carefully until you understand it:

> To locate your dominant, look to the fourth letter of your personality type (J or P). This will tell you how you extravert, whether with your perceiving function (S or N) or with your judging function (T or F). Then look at the first letter (E or I) of your personality type. If you prefer Extraversion, how you extravert will be your dominant function. If you prefer Introversion, then the other letter will be your dominant.

For example, for ESTJ, the last letter (J) points to the judging function, which is T; since this person is an Extravert, T is the dominant function, with S as the auxiliary. In an opposite example, INFP, the last letter (P) points to the perceiving function, which is N; that is how this person extraverts. However, since this person prefers Introversion, the F is the introverted dominant function and N is the auxiliary.

Our dominant function is important to our spirituality because it will lead us as we prepare for the journey, as we navigate the journey, and as we reengage with the elements of our faith along the way. But it will be refined and balanced for a greater wholeness in collaboration with the auxiliary. In order to include all four mental functions (S, N, T, and F), Jung established a hierarchy that he labeled the dominant, auxiliary, tertiary, and inferior functions. The tertiary function is usually much less developed and conscious than the first two. It is the opposite of the auxiliary. The inferior function, the opposite of the dominant function, has received the least energy and attention and therefore is the least developed. According to Jungian theory, the inferior function is the primary connection to the unconscious and the most difficult to use in one's conscious life. Under stress or crisis, when our dominant is not coping well in our conscious life, often the inferior will kick in, bringing with it lots of chaotic perceptions or judgments. At this point people will see us at our worst.

Our less-preferred functions, especially the inferior, are vital to integrate the self because they access the rich depth available in the unconscious. The inferior function is therefore our greatest source for learning about new sides of ourselves and alternative potentialities to complement those strengths we currently possess. Avenues for spiritual growth are discovered in those moments when we are off balance and vulnerable. In these moments great insights for personal and spiritual growth arise.

When people are young, their energy is directed toward development of their most preferred, dominant function, and their behavior reflects this. For example, an introverted Feeling child will be a quiet observer, with an instinctive sense of others' feelings; an introverted Intuitive child will be actively exploring the variety of the surrounding world. An extraverted Thinking child will try to order his environment to fit with his logical principles; an introverted Thinking child will try to internally make sense of her world. Once children develop skills in their dominant function, the focus of energy and attention then shifts to the auxiliary function. The primary task of type development in the first part of life is to establish the leadership provided by the dominant function, balanced by the healthy development of the auxiliary function. Later in life, the focus of development shifts, this time to the less-preferred functions, aspects of the individual's personality and potential that have only minimally been explored. This redirection of energy is part of the midlife transition, which Jung saw as the gateway to later life development and satisfaction. The task of the second half of life, then, is to move toward full development of all of oneself, including those parts that were previously neglected and unrealized.

When people first learn Jung's theory, they often think the ideal is to develop all four functions with equal facility to achieve balance. That, however, is not how development works, for if a person tries to develop opposite ways of perceiving equally, for example, then neither Sensing nor Intuition will receive the focus or attention necessary to become fully reliable. The four functions tend to pull in opposite directions: Sensing, to the reality of the present; Intuition, to the possibility of the future; Thinking, to decisions based on objective logic; and Feeling, to decisions based on subjective values. People who do not establish dominance of each pair of functions are inconsistent in their behavior, pulled first in one direction and then another. The goal of type development, then, is not equal development and use of all the functions, but rather the ability to use each mental process with some facility when it is appropriate.

Using combinations of preferences yields interesting results on the topic of learning styles. Combining the first two letters of your type reveals some interesting patterns. The first two letters show where you prefer to focus your attention and how you prefer to take in information. For example, ES types are usually more interested in the practical usefulness of learning, while IN types are usually more interested in abstractions and learning for its own sake. Using the second and last letters of one's type is also a useful way to think about learning style. The second letter (S or N) describes whether one prefers to focus on facts and reality (Sensing) or abstract concepts and theories (Intuition). The last letter (J or P) indicates whether one prefers to decide on that information quickly and then move on (Judging) or keep open to new information (Perceiving).

As helpful as it is to know our personality type—as that of our spouse, siblings, co-workers, and friends—and as much as our personality type impacts our life and preferences, we must not forget that other factors are also influential and possibly even determinative of our lifestyle, behavior, and storyline. These factors include such experiences as upbringing, schooling, life lessons, social status, religious values and teaching, failures, accomplishments, talents, abilities, interests, intelligence, adaptability, and openness to growth and change.

Spirituality Types

Personality and spirituality are deeply interrelated, so much that neither function adequately apart from the other. Like cyclists on a tandem, personality and spirituality travel together through the journey of life. Riding in tandem, they are deeply influenced by conditions both internal (goals, moods, desires) and external to the self. When one leans, the other leans; where one starts, the other starts; if one stops, the other stops. Though not identical, they strive to be in sync, balancing one another in profound and intimate ways. Personality takes the lead, and where personality goes, spirituality follows, though not blindly or passively. Spirituality has its own voice, and when its desires are addressed and heeded, personality thrives. When the two disagree, they must communicate, or the consequences can be disastrous. Cooperation always enhances the ride.

Building on the insights of psychological type theory developed by Carl Jung and Isabel Briggs Myer, Peter Tufts Richardson notes that four different approaches to human spirituality emerge from the MBTI.[2] How we perceive the world and how we respond to it (how we judge) seems to be directly connected to the spiritual path we find most personally satisfying. Utilizing the principle that one's spirituality flows out of one's individuality, Richardson locates the key to spirituality in the two middle letters of one's personality type. These cognitive pairs result in four possibilities: ST, SF, NT, and NF. One of these pairs defines each person's spirituality.

STs, for example, are characterized by a *task-oriented spirituality*. ST youth are drawn to activities that are task-oriented, such as team sports. And often they will be leaders. They learn by experience, wanting to discover things for themselves; they need to know why things are required and how they work. As teens STs divide into two groups: the freedom lovers (STPs) and the responsible ones (STJs), but all are oriented around well-defined institutions. When they grow up, STs become the realists, always in touch with the facts, unbiased, objective, accurate, paying attention to relevant details. They are skilled administrators, responsible, consistent, efficient, and analytical.

STs commit themselves to the building up and maintaining of institutions, reliably and loyally. They prefer direct, experience-based, often physical activities, working with their hands or otherwise directly in situations, trying out procedures to see what works best, often preferring technical

2. Richardson's approach is described in *Four Spiritualities*.

tasks to those requiring people skills. They learn best on the job, noticing relevant details, collecting facts, and verifying them directly by the senses. They arrive at conclusions in a linear cause-and-effect way. Their opinions, based on their experience, will often be firmly held and based on common sense. A confusion of beliefs is intolerable for STs. They like to find a world in balance, with reliable structures that lead them toward the right way to go. For the Journey of Works, order and a clear message are essential conditions. Appreciating clear beliefs and reliable structure, they tend to be literalists and legalists in religion; commitment provides religion stability.

SFs are characterized by an *experience-based spirituality*. SF youth make friends easily, avoid conflict, and desire to please. They thrive in well-structured environments and when expectations are clear. They need to be reassured when they are on the right track and rewarded for good behavior. As adults SFs are sensitive, loyal, and caring; they live responsibly as parents and citizens and are devoted to serving others in tangible ways. Instead of the cosmic, the tangible task at hand is the focus. Details are important. Stressing continuity and propriety, SFs are traditionalists. In their communications they prefer anecdotes, stories, and tangible references to symbolic or abstract reasoning. Practical and interactive, they take a tactile, hands-on approach to the spiritual life.

NTs are characterized by a *highly principled spirituality*. NT youth value their independence and tend to work hard to establish their competence in the challenges they decide to tackle. Uncomfortable with abstraction, they often ask why, and if the answers they receive are unsatisfactory, they may set out to improve upon them or else to rebel against arbitrary answers. As adults NTs tend to enjoy solving problems, love to exchange ideas, or stimulate new efforts. Searching for unifying solutions, they appreciate speculative theories that lead to intellectual clarity. NTs are foremost change agents and strategic planners. On account of their critical nature, they may be perceived by others, particularly SFs, as stubborn or uncooperative. Along with principles and truth, individuals on this path are also distinguished by vision and concern for social justice.

NFs are characterized by a *questing spirituality*. NF youth like to please the adults and peers in their lives. They can be easily crushed by disapproval or even indifference. They need regular affirmation from parents and teachers if their self-esteem and self-image are not to suffer. Because they see possibilities in the future (N) and like to gain approval from others, they often will prepare for careers and causes in response to adult mentors in their lives. NF youth are exceedingly idealistic. Their idealism is often unpredictable; some young men may overcompensate for their F by expressing their idealism in hostile ways. They are strongly represented among protestors for social issues. NF adults are enthusiastic and insightful, recognizing the personal needs of others. Idealists by nature, they always see a way to make life better. They have an ability to draw people into a discussion and to facilitate consensus-building for social harmony and good. NFs on a healthy track will regularly draw others toward their own best selves. The Intuitive proclivity for symbol and metaphor, combining with global vision for the well-being of the world, makes NFs inspired communicators of the ideal. Future-oriented and attuned to the big picture of life as a whole, NFs tend to focus more on possibilities than on concrete situations at hand. Their N nature is balanced, however, by their F side, which keeps them in touch with reality and keeps their utopian bent in check. Flexible and open to change, NFs see life as continual self-creating process, a quest toward selfhood. Their malleable natures exist to be formed and re-formed in ever more exquisite patterns of self-actualization. NFs seek increasing meaning and spiritual purpose in life.

Urban Holmes, Dean of the School of Theology at The University of the South in Sewanee, Tennessee from 1973 until his death in 1981, presents a helpful typology for the spiritual life in his insightful book *A History of Spirituality*. His book provides a tool and a method by which to conceptualize and name spiritual experience within a basic framework, particularly useful in helping to position one's own religious experience within the context of the experience of others.

Aware that spirituality is shaped by personality and unique to each individual, but also that "birds of a feather flock together," Holmes presents a helpful typology for the spiritual life revolving around four ways that people seek to understand the experience of God and its meaning for our times:

- Type I: sacramental (an intellectual, "thinking" spirituality)
- Type II: charismatic (a heartfelt, intuitive spirituality)
- Type III: mystical (a contemplative, introspective spirituality)
- Type IV: apostolic (an active, visionary spirituality)

Holmes calls his model the "Circle of Sensibility," and in it he delineates four styles of prayer, later configured as schools of spirituality. By "sensibility" he refers to the possibilities within individuals and communities as they seek to understand the experience of God and its meaning for our times. Holmes proposes the use of two intersecting lines placed within a circle. The vertical line creates a north-south axis, with Sensibility (Mind or Intellect) at the north pole and Affective (Heart or Emotion) at the south pole. The horizontal line creates an east-west axis, with Kataphatic (God as Revealed: known through images) at the east pole and Apophatic (God as Mystery: known mystically). His circle, divided into four quadrants, contains four schools of spirituality, which he labeled "speculative-kataphatic" (Type I spirituality), affective-kataphatic (Type II spirituality), affective-apophatic (Type III spirituality), and speculative-apophatic (Type IV spirituality).

Holmes's typology overlaps significantly with Jung's typology, as incorporated in the MBTI. Type I spirituality, an intellectual "thinking" spirituality, has been identified as "sacramental." Its primary aim is to aid persons in fulfilling their vocation in the world. This spirituality favors what it can see, touch, and vividly imagine. Type II spirituality, a sensate, heartfelt approach to spirituality, has been identified as "charismatic." Its primary aim is to achieve holiness of life through personal renewal. Type III spirituality, which emphasizes being and direct experience of God, has been identified as "mystical." Its primary aim is union with the Holy, an unattainable goal, a journey that nevertheless continually impels the disciple onward. Type IV spirituality, a visionary, almost crusading type of spirituality, has been identified as "apostolic." Its primary aim is to obey God's will completely. Its major concerns are witness to God's reign and striving for justice and peace.

Many studies identify the Jungian typology with the four schools of spirituality. Typically they place "STs" in the speculative-kataphatic school, the "SFs" in the affective-kataphatic, the "NFs" in the affective-apophatic, and the "NTs" in the speculative-apophatic. In his work *Spiritual Life*, theologian John Westerhoff suggests an alternative approach, namely, following Jung's contention that only the stronger of the two middle traits is a useful indicator of behavior.[3] According to this insight, there are four categories available: T, S, N, and F. Adhering to this paradigm, the schools of spirituality and personality types look like this: Type I spirituality (speculative-kataphatic) = S; Type II spirituality (affective-kataphatic) = F; Type III spirituality (affective-apophatic) = N; and Type IV spirituality (speculative-apophatic) = T. According to this approach, the area of primary growth is indicated by one's diagonal spirituality type. For example, the needs of Type

3. Westerhoff, *Spiritual Life*, 61.

II spirituality are complemented by Type IV spirituality, and those of Type III by Type I, and vice versa. While one school of spirituality may initially meet one's personality needs, that person's diagonal spirituality type along the circle of sensibility represents his/her growing edge.

Having provided an understanding of personality types and their connection to spirituality types, we may now see how this framework lays the groundwork for the stories told in *Our Exodus Story*. As noted in the preface, each of our four protagonists exhibits distinct dominant personality characteristics. As you will discover, of our mirror twins, Georgia and Helen, one is an N, the other an F; and one spouse is an S, while the other is a T. How different individuals can exhibit uniquely diverse dominant personality categories and yet work together, sharing partnership commitment while maintaining individual wholeness, integrity, and joy, is the story of their lives, uniquely and jointly expressed in the following chapters.

As Jungian author Herman Hesse displays in his Nobel Prize-winning novels, described variously as "spiritual autobiographies" or as "biographies of the soul," what Christians call "salvation"—a process known alternatively as enlightenment, wholeness, integration, fulfillment, harmony, clarity, or awareness—may be gained, achieved, or affirmed through a combination of factors or in a variety of ways. What is clear is that there is no single paradigm, formula, or avenue for achieving this goal or state of grace. While salvation is a divine gift, labeled variously as "original blessing" or primal wholeness, it must be reclaimed individually, utilizing one of four primary ways of functioning—sensing, intuiting, thinking, and feeling—with talents and inclinations typical of artisans (sensors and designers), mystics (poets and artists), thinkers (scientists, mathematicians, philosophers, and theologians), and feelers (caregivers and guardians), relying on one or more of the four dimensions of the self, namely, the body and one's senses, the spirit or one's imagination, the mind and one's intellectual capacity, and the soul or one's emotional resources.

Characteristics of Fully Developed Human Beings

Richard Coan, a professor of psychology at the University of Arizona, spent a large part of his professional career seeking to determine the nature of the optimal human personality. He provides a survey of his findings in his 1977 book *Hero, Artist, Sage or Saint?* Coan begins by showing that psychology as a science cannot provide the goals for human life. He claims that if any goals are provided by psychology, the psychologists must either introduce them surreptitiously or openly acknowledge the need for religion and transpersonal meaning.

Coan concludes that there are five elements that characterize the fully developed human person: efficiency, creativity, inner harmony, relatedness, and transcendence. As Coan describes these elements, he defines efficiency as the heroic quality. Heroes accomplish things with effectiveness, have strong egos, and are able to focus the direction of their lives. The second element, creativity, is often represented by artists, who are able to present images, poetry, or ideas in a new way so that they touch others with a dimension beyond the physical. The third element is embodied by the sage, the person who has achieved inner harmony. The fourth and fifth elements, relatedness and transcendence, are manifested by the saint, the person who treats others with understanding, caring, love, empathy, social sensitivity, and compassion. Saints make other people feel loved and enable them to love. While relatedness may be considered the horizontal aspect of saintliness, transcendence is the vertical aspect of saintliness.

Coan suggests that Carl Jung best integrated these concerns in his theory and practice, developing a framework in which all of these have a place. Using Jungian terminology, the following correlations seem likely, starting with the four dominant functions of the personality, continuing with the four dimensions of the self, and proceeding with Coan's elements of fully developed persons:

- sensing: body/senses; acting (artisans, heroes)
- intuiting: spirit/imagination; creating (artists, poets)
- thinking: mind/intellect; discerning (philosophers, sages)
- feeling: soul/heart; caring (caregivers, saints)

In writing his novel *Siddhartha*, Hesse came to the realization that we honor our spiritual mentors—be they the Buddha, Muhammad, Moses, or Jesus Christ—not through devotion to their dogma but by following their example. This teaching is central to the Buddhist Theravada tradition, which holds that the path to enlightenment is a solitary one, and that no person can lead another to self-understanding. Creeds and dogmas can be helpful guides, but each person's spiritual path is unknowable up front. Thus, it is up to each person to discover the way, intuitively and indirectly, from small clues experience provides along the way. When, at the book's end, Govinda asks Siddhartha, "Do you have a doctrine? Is there a belief or some knowledge that guides you, that helps you to live and do what is right?" Siddhartha replies, "I have had thoughts, yes, and insights, now and again . . . Here is one of the thoughts I have found: Wisdom cannot be passed on. Wisdom that a wise man attempts to pass on always sounds like foolishness."[4]

Siddhartha ultimately understands that the essence of enlightenment already exists within each person, and that it is present in the world at all times. Prescriptive paths simply lead people further from themselves and from the wisdom they seek. An indirect approach is more likely to take into account therapeutic resources in the world and is therefore better able to provide the necessary distance from which to apprehend the unity of the world. On his journey, Siddhartha finds that wholeness comes not from mastery of either material or spiritual reality but from finding the common ground between these polarities of existence. The river, with its opposing banks, represents the polarities, and the river itself represents their ideal union. Siddhartha achieves transcendence when he can accept that all is false and true at the same time, that all is simultaneously living and dead, and that all possibilities are present in the universe, ready to reveal themselves to us when we are willing and able to receive them.

As Hesse discovered in the Buddhist Theravada tradition, enlightenment is achieved, not by worshipping the Buddha or the Christ as a god, but rather through yielding, detachment, nonaction, and letting go. As Jesus also taught, while the way to blessedness and contentment is through compassion and love, ultimately, bliss is experienced not by knowing or doing but simply by being. In Hesse's novel, an individual's experience—the totality of conscious events of a human life, including sensing, intuiting, thinking, and feeling—is the best way to approach understanding of reality and to attain enlightenment. Such understanding is attained neither through intellectual methods (knowing) nor through physical pleasure (doing), but rather by the entirety of life's experiences—mentally, emotionally, physically, and spiritually. Individually, events are meaningless in themselves, but taken together, they can lead to understanding.

As noted above, the MBTI charts sixteen relatively stable personality types, based on individual preferences. This does not mean, however, that these preferences cannot change over time. In midlife, for example, many people experience what is dramatically termed "the midlife crisis," when the self undergoes transformation, "crossing over" from one psychological

4. Hesse, *Siddhartha*, 118–19.

identity to another. While some individuals experience extensive internal restructuring at this time, others experience a defensive retreat into former patterns of identity.

As we reflect on the psychological purpose of the midlife transition, precipitated by a combination of internal and external factors and circumstances, what is clear is that a change in preferences, and therefore in personality type, ushers some individuals into what is often called their second half of life spirituality, when they enter the years of mature adulthood and some of them the period of mature spirituality. One of the major tasks of persons in the second half of life is to identify ways of staying effectively in touch with ongoing change, transformation, and liminality.

According to Jungian personality theory, each person has a dominant function, a captain or home base of operations, and a first mate or auxiliary function, their second most important function. However, as there are times in a ship's journey when the second and third mates may need to assume dominance or leadership over the captain and first mate, so in midlife or during our second half of life, our personality preferences may shift from our dominant to our auxiliary or even to our tertiary or inferior functions, which, as we have seen, complement the strengths we currently possess and are vital to integrate the self because they access the rich depth available in our unconscious. In addition, they represent significant avenues for spiritual growth, since they are utilized in those moments when we are off balance and in vulnerable moments when great insights for personal and spiritual growth often arise. Better yet, wholeness is achieved when all four functions are integrated and fully alive in a harmonious way. Such unity, both healing and transformative, is indicative of spiritual maturity.

Fritz Pearls, founder of Gestalt psychology, called the parts in us that function as opposites of how we prefer to think or act "polarities." Carl Jung called this disowned material "the shadow self." According to Jung, one's shadow includes "good" qualities as well as "bad" or "shameful" qualities that one denies. As we make room for our polarities, we become healthier and more open to transforming grace.

In his bestselling counter-cultural novel *Steppenwolf*, Hesse presents a severely fractured individual named Harry Haller, whose divided personality is described as being half man and half wolf, a highly principled individual driven by an intellectual (thinking) sensibility who hates the bourgeois lifestyle but who at the same time is incapable of surrendering himself to the pleasures of the senses. As Hesse describes him, Henry consists of multiple identities, evidence of the multifaceted nature of the human soul, something that for Hesse is true not only of Harry but is an inherent condition of all humans.

In *Steppenwolf*, Harry is taken to his metaphorical "magic theater," where he discovers facets of his personality that had long been hidden. In the Magic Theater Harry learns that like other human beings, he is comprised of innumerable selves that may be reconfigured in varying ways, like chess pieces.

While we might artificially categorize people as uniquely aesthetic, artistic, philosophic, and mystical—with overlap in most cases, since few people are one-dimensional—we must note that for Hesse, none is inherently higher spiritually than another. One can be deeply spiritual and spiritually fulfilled as artist, poet, thinker, or mystic. For this reason, the distinction frequently made between people in their spiritual first or second half of lives appears inadequate, since it seems evident that people can be fulfilled spiritually in first half of life spirituality (that is, living securely under rules and with clear boundary markers—ways of living and thinking described as precritical or as one's first naiveté) as authentically as in second half of life spirituality (that is, living maturely without rules or clear boundary markers—ways of living and thinking described as postcritical or as one's second naiveté). However, because second half of life seekers are willing to take risks and are more fully open to ambiguity and mystery, they tend to be less assertive, combative, dogmatic, and possessive and more open to change, qualities reflecting a higher and fuller dimension of spirituality.

3

Mirror Twins

WHILE MULTIPLE BIRTHS OR litters are natural among many animal species, the common offspring pattern for humans is a single birth, normally following a nine-month pregnancy. Despite the prevalence of this pattern, human mothers sometimes give birth to multiple children simultaneously, from twins up to a record nine births, called nonuplets. With the use of reproductive technology such as fertility drugs and in vitro fertilization, the births of twins and triplets have become increasingly common.

The Biology behind the Birth of Twins

On a global scale, the odds of a mother giving natural birth to twins are approximately 1 to 250. In the United States, twins account for about 3 percent of live births. As is commonly known, not all twins are alike. While there are many different kinds of twins, due to a variety of biological processes and possibilities, at birth the most common are fraternal and identical twins.

Fraternal twins, also called dizygotic twins, are the result of two separate eggs being fertilized by two separate sperm. This can happen when a woman's ovaries release two eggs instead of one. Fraternal twins can be as alike or unalike as siblings; in other words, they are not identical. Fraternal twins might be two boys, two girls, or a boy and a girl. Each fetus develops in his or her own placenta.

Identical twins, or monozygotic twins, form when one fertilized egg splits in two and grows into two separate embryos. In this case, some twins are the same gender, share the same blood type, and share the same physical traits. Identical twins may or may not share one amniotic sac. While identical twins have the same DNA at birth, eventually the DNA becomes more distinctive over time, based on environmental factors. For example, one twin can become heterosexual and the other homosexual. Likewise, each can develop different and even contrasting personality qualities and types. Due to socialization, each twin evolves to be a unique individual.

In the case of conjoined twins, sometimes called Siamese twins, the embryo only partially separates, and the two fetuses remain partially connected, both before birth and as they grow after birth. Conjoined twins connect at different spots, including the chest, abdomen, or hips. Such twins may also share one or more internal organs. Sadly, many conjoined twins do not survive to full term, or live only briefly after birth. Conjoined twins who do survive are sometimes successfully separated by surgery. Such twins may share the placenta (the organ that connects the mother and baby), amniotic sac (the inner membranes), and chorion (the outer membrane), but sometimes they have their own.

While a couple's chances of having twins depends on many factors, research shows that some people are at a higher likelihood of having twins than others. For example, women who are fraternal twins have a 1 in 60 chance of having twins, and men who are fraternal twins have a 1 in 125 chance of fathering twins. Whereas in the past it was believed that identical twins are random, family history may increase one's chances of monozygotic twinning. However, the chances of having identical twins run in a family are rare: only around 3 or 4 in every 1,000 births are identical twins.

Since the birth of fraternal twins involves the female contributing extra eggs during ovulation, male members would not be responsible for such occurrences. However, if one's family has a history of twins but seems to have skipped a generation, the likely case is that the person who carried the so-called twin genes that generation was male.

Other factors contributing to the birth of twins involve age (women over the age of thirty, especially in their late thirties, have an increased chance of twin pregnancies, particularly if they have previously given births); race (certain races, particularly Black or African-American women, unlike women of Japanese ancestry, who have the lowest prevalence of twins); weight and height (women who are taller and heavier or both are more likely to have twins); prior twin pregnancies; and fertility treatments (the latter two factors are known to increase the chances of multiple eggs being released and fertilized).

Georgia and Helen's Ancestral History (Maternal)

Georgia and Helen are monozygotic twins: Georgia is right-handed and Helen is left-handed. The common name for this type of twin is "mirror twins," for they are identical, like looking in a mirror. Their account starts with their French-Canadian maternal ancestors in the eastern and midwestern states of Virginia, Illinois, and Oklahoma, and their paternal ancestors in England and Lithuania.

Their earliest ancestral remembrance goes back to their maternal grandmother Georgia Dickens Brinley, born in 1903 to Victoria and George Dickens, the latter a physician related to the novelist Charles Dickens. Victoria, a member of the Seymour family of Illinois, was the daughter of Mahala and Frank Seymour. Our story begins a generation earlier, with Mahala's father Jacques and Mary Schifflet. Jacques Schifflet, a French Canadian of pure French ancestry, had come from Canada to the United States in the 1830s, when he began working on a plantation in Virginia. He married Mary and in 1840 had a son, John. In 1843 their second child was born, a daughter named Mahala. The occasion was both joyous and tragic, for Mary died in childbirth. Shortly thereafter, Jacques remarried, and eventually had a second daughter, named Charlotte.

Like many men of his generation, Jacques was an inveterate gambler, and he and his friends gathered often to pursue their vice. Guns were always present, in case anyone got out of line. While gambling is rarely profitable, Jacques used it to his advantage, to the point of acquiring a sizeable fortune, which he used to purchase his boss's plantation. As youngsters, John and Mahala helped out with the chores, John with plantation work and Mahala around the house.

Around the age of sixteen, John became involved in his father's mule-breeding business, taking mules and slaves to New Orleans and traveling from there to St. Louis to sell their merchandise. As a young teenager, Mahala often accompanied her brother on these business trips, enjoying the travel. However, she detested the slave trade, and went shopping when John conducted business. This took place shortly before the Civil War.

At home, Mahala found disfavor with her stepmother, for Mahala was high spirited and they clashed on many points. On one occasion Mahala ran away from home, going to a nearby town, where she found work in a minister's home. Jacques sent workers to track her down and she was found doing housework at the minister's home, where she was apprehended and brought back home. Within a year, the Civil War broke out, at which time Mahala left home again, never to return. During the Civil War, people of wealth often hid their gold coins and jewelry in the yard, burying it for safekeeping for fear that bands of soldiers might take it. Eventually, John and Mahala were given three gold pieces each, as a dowry or for use in emergencies.[1]

During the fighting, John, unwilling to fight for the South, also left home, traveling northwest to Ohio and later to Illinois. When Jacques was called to fight for the South, he was able to send a slave in his place, as was common. When that person died or deserted, Jacques sent another slave, who also disappeared on the battlefield, and this finally forced Jacques to serve as a soldier. Having lived a life of leisure, he soon succumbed to pneumonia and died on the field of battle, in an unmarked grave.

Meanwhile, Mahala followed her brother north, joining him in Circleville, Ohio, where John had met and married a local girl. Mahala was sixteen years old at the time, and she soon met and married Francis (Frank) Seymour in his hometown of Peoria, Illinois. Seymour had come from England, having been born in Cornwall in 1834. After completing an engineering degree, he migrated to the United States, where he worked as a mine surveyor. He traveled widely at this time, surveying over fifty coal mines in Ohio, Indiana, and Illinois. Eventually he moved to Oklahoma, dying in 1906.

Over the years, Mahala and Frank had thirteen children, including one set of twins. As happened all too often at that time, some of the children died in childhood, whether at birth, through tragic accidents, or from terminal illness. Only four lived to maturity. The twins, named Victoria (1879–1952) and Eudora, were the last born. Of these, only Victoria grew to adulthood, for her twin died of dysentery in childhood, at three months of age. The twins had been born in Colfax, Illinois, where Frank had discovered what was then the deepest mine in the country. From Illinois, Frank traveled to Missouri and eventually to Oklahoma, laying mines along the way.

1. Mahala's three gold pieces were passed on to Georgia Ann Brinley, who used one of her $2½ gold pieces as bail to get a friend out of jail, and was never paid back. One was passed down to Georgia, an heirloom she is keeping for her nephew (and Helen's grandson) Tyler.

When Victoria was nineteen, she settled with her family in McAlester, Oklahoma, where she ran a hotel with her mother, something they had done in Illinois as well, while Frank and the male children laid mines. In 1902 Victoria married the physician George Dickens, related to novelist Charles Dickens on his father's side but to a mother of Melungeon ancestry (a term for people of mixed ancestry in Southeastern United States) named Mary Frances Polk (1856–1924), related by birth to James Knox Polk (American president from 1845–1849). Their union resulted in the birth of Georgia Adaline Dickens, Georgia and Helen's maternal grandmother, in 1903, but also in a short marriage, for Victoria and George were divorced in 1906. Around that time, Mahala and Victoria's hotel burned down, and Victoria returned with her family to Illinois, while George Dickens stayed in Oklahoma.

While in high school in Benton, Illinois, Georgia Adaline (1903–1996) Dickens met William Brinley Jr. (1904–1969), whose family was also in the mining business. At Benton High, she saw William being cuffed on the head with a book by his teacher and she instantly fell in love. As a young teenager in high school, William worked part-time in a mine and as a result, eventually contracted black lung disease. Georgia married William in 1922, shortly after graduating from high school, before relocating to western Pennsylvania in 1925, where William Jr. joined his father in the mines as safety Superintendent.

Mine safety was strongly emphasized in mining communities during the 1930s and 1940s. Safety was stressed daily and safety teams were formed at western Pennsylvania mines to administer first aid in the event of accidents. Teams from various mines would get together periodically and compete to see which team could provide the quickest and most effective first aid for simulated accidents. However, despite the many safety precautions, the coal mine was still a dangerous place to work and accidents happened regularly. Despite the emphasis on safety, it is hard to visualize the conditions that miners faced in their everyday work back then. First or all, it was pitch dark hundreds of feet below ground level. There were no lights other than the small battery powered light on the miner's hard hat. At the workplace, the air was extremely dusty from the cutting and blasting, and barely breathable. The miners worked in the atmosphere all day without any face masks. However, for new immigrants and those working during the depression years, men were happy to have a job that paid steady wages.

Life in mine homes was quite chaotic. Families were large, with lots of children sleeping together, often three or more to a room. Babies were regularly delivered at home, with the help of neighbor midwives. Young men often started working at the age of eighteen. One group of miners would leave early in the morning and return at 3 p.m. Another group would leave at 3:00, returning home late at night. It was not uncommon for fathers and sons to work different shifts. Workers would emerge from the mines covered with coal dust. The only running water was from a common pump outside, and the bathroom was an outhouse behind the house. With no indoor plumbing, returning miners would wash themselves by kneeling before a large tub filled with water from the outdoor pump. Women would arise at 4 a.m. to pump water on wash day before the town's well went dry that day.

Mining continued during the years of the Great Depression, employing many workers and contributing to the country's recovery and to the great war effort that followed. In the 1930s, miners at the Morgan mine were fortunate to work three or four days a week. Everyone in town would wait at five o'clock to listen for the siren at the mine to sound. This was the signal that there would be work the next day at the mine.

In 1925, the senior Brinleys moved to Muse, a small mining town twenty-five miles southwest of Pittsburgh and three miles north of Canonsburg, where William Sr worked for the National Mining Company at National No. 3 mine as Superintendent until his death in 1933. Meanwhile, his wife Mauretta worked in payroll at the Muse mine. However, having grown up Methodist in the Midwest, she had trouble adapting to the mining culture of Pennsylvania, Irish, Italian, and Eastern European in nature and predominantly Roman Catholic. Some miners were Protestant, of course, as were many mine administrators and residents nearby such as farmers and small business owners. Over the years, towns and villages in southwestern Pennsylvania erected Catholic churches near Presbyterian, Methodist, Baptist, and Lutheran churches, often on opposite corners or across the street from one another.

While the senior Brinleys lived and worked in Muse, William Jr. and Georgia Adaline Brinley lived in the nearby mining town of Morgan, where William Jr. worked for the National Mining Company at National No. 1 mine as mine Superintendent. Their home in Morgan, located a few hundred yards from the mine portal, was one of four homes on supervisor's row, one for Irish workers, another for Italian workers, a third for Polish workers, and the fourth for William Brinley, mine Superintendent. It was in that home, currently owned and occupied by Bob and Helen Benson, that their only child, Georgia Ann Brinley, was born (1937–2015). Nearby were homes for the miners, the Italian club, the company store, a gas station, a truck stop or diner called Twigs, a bar named "The Hideaway," a ballpark, and an elementary school with a store nearby, where schoolchildren went during recess to buy candy.

Towns like Morgan had no churches of their own. Lacking transportation, Catholic families walked along railroad tracks to Bridgeville for Mass. For shopping or entertainment, people took the Wabash train line to Pittsburgh. Passenger trains came through Morgan in the morning and again in the evening. Most mining communities had a company store, and Morgan was no exception. Company stores were divided into numerous departments, offering sufficient merchandise in each department to supply residents with most needs. Like mini-Wal-Marts, these stores carried everything from furniture and clothing to food, ice cream, and penny candy trays. Charges would be checked for credit, then entered on a worker's charge card account. During the 1920s and 1930s, company stores had a captive market, and workers and their families bought most of their groceries and other needs there. Company stores were gathering points for many of the townspeople and youth. When the mines shut down, supermarkets, mom and pop stores, and malls eventually replaced the company stores as places to shop and mingle.

Most of the miners' homes were duplexes. They were owned by the mining company, which charged a modest rent, withholding payment from the miners' wages. After World War II, the houses were sold to a real estate firm, and then resold to the people who lived in them. They offered good bargains at that time, with one half of a duplex selling for approximately $1300–$2500 if bought on credit–at a time when wages were 55 to 60 cents an hour. After the houses became privately owned, the new owners took pride in their homes, maintaining a good appearance for the neighborhood.

When the mining industry in western Pennsylvania began to decline after World War II, leading to the collapse of the U.S. Steel industry in the late 1970s and early 1980s, some workers relocated or abandoned their homes. These trends further depressed southwestern Pennsylvania's small, rural mining towns. As people born, raised, and educated in these communities began moving out, the federal government created newly-built public housing projects intended for lower income families, some of them

African American. These neighborhood projects had low-income limits, and mortgages or rates were subsidized with federal projects. Over time, the people of Morgan, like those in other rural Appalachian communities, either suffered further depression from mining decline or learned to be enriched by the social, economic, and religious diversity stemming from multicultural immersion.

When mining jobs began disappearing, exacerbated by greater awareness of mental and physical disorders, coupled with climate change and increasing antipollution ordinances, mining careers and related industrial changes left mining families feeling vulnerable and insecure. In addition to difficult mining conditions, which contributed to lung and respiratory ailments and shortened life expectancy, the mine culture contributed to dysfunctional family life, class and race conflicts, violent behavior, depression, and suicide. Such factors certainly impacted incidents of alcoholism, drug dependency, and other addictive problems in communities across the Appalachian region, particularly in southwestern Pennsylvania, West Virginia, and western Virginia, where illicit drug use soared in the 1980s and beyond, including the proliferation of cocaine, crack, heroin, methamphetamines, and prescription drugs such as OxyContin. Opioid abuse and overdose deaths in the United States continued in the twenty-first century generally but particularly in the Appalachian region, and they continue to afflict current and previous mining communities disproportionately.

During World War II, William Brinley was too old for conscription, but insisted on participating in the war effort by joining the Seabees, the naval construction force. In addition to construction work on the European field of battle, his job also included gathering dead bodies from the field of battle.

As mine Superintendent, William was well connected socially. Earlier, he had known John L. Lewis, president of the United Mine Workers of America (UMWA) union from 1920 to 1960, and later he participated in Friday evening card games with UMWA president Tony Boyle (president from 1963 until 1972).

From the beginning of his tenure, Boyle faced significant opposition from rank-and-file miners and UMWA leaders. Over time, miners' attitudes about their union had changed. Miners wanted greater democracy and more local autonomy for their local unions. There was widespread belief that Boyle was more concerned with protecting mine owners' interests than those of his members. Grievances filed by the union often took years to resolve, lending credence to the miners' claim. Wildcat strikes occurred as local unions, despairing of UMWA assistance, sought to resolve local disputes with walkouts.

In 1974, Boyle was convicted of charges of conspiracy in the murder of Joseph A. "Jock" Yablonski, Yablonski's wife Margaret, and their daughter Charlotte on New Year's Eve, December 31, 1969. Running against Boyle for president of the United Mine Workers union, Yablonski had accused Boyle of embezzling from the union funds and for taking kickbacks from mine owners to get reelected. After losing the election, Yablonski also charged that fraud had been committed. After the murder of Yablonski and his family members, the hired murderers were found, and two years later Boyle was indicted and sentenced to three life terms, dying while still incarcerated.

King Coal and Mine Culture in Southwestern Pennsylvania

The small town of Morgan (current population is 287), an unincorporated community in South Fayette Township, is located ten miles southwest of Pittsburgh and two miles west of Bridgeville. Today, South Fayette is a fast-growing community benefitting from its proximity to downtown Pittsburgh, a corporate center called Southpointe, Pittsburgh International Airport, and a highly ranked school district. In 2013, South Fayette was nominated in a regional survey as the best Pittsburgh suburb in which to raise a family.

The earliest known settler was a man of English descent with the surname Miller, who came to the area about 1768. He settled at the mouth of a stream that would be named Millers Run (this spot is currently north of Bridgeville, where the stream joins Chartiers Creek, which flows north until it empties into the Ohio River five miles below Pittsburgh near McKees Rocks). Land was plentiful then, and settlers competed with Indians and wild animals for survival. Before later emigrating to Kentucky, Miller sold an expansive tract of land to a speculator for a pair of shoes. In 1790, Captain Samuel Morgan (for whom the town of Morgan is named) built a gristmill on Millers Run, later purchased by Moses Coulter, whose son converted it into a steam mill. He added a sawmill and later changed it to a steel mill. Coal and oil were discovered in the township between 1860 and 1910, and mining became an important industry.

Pennsylvania has a long and rich coal mining history dating to the 1700s. Anthracite, or hard coal, was mined in the eastern part of the state as early as 1775, while bituminous, or soft coal, was mined in western Pennsylvania beginning around 1760. Pennsylvania coal has been used to generated power, heat homes, and produce steel, among other uses. Pennsylvania coal also helped power the Industrial Revolution and helped the United States win two world wars. In the early 1900s, southwestern Pennsylvania became a Mecca for coal mines, which were a major factor in making Pittsburgh the steel mill capital of the world. Morgan's National No. 1 mine, owned by the National Mining Company, opened around 1903, providing work for thousands of families until its closing in the early 1950s. While mining activity in Pennsylvania peaked during the early twentieth century, there are still over forty underground mines actively mining coal in Pennsylvania, as well as five thousand or more abandoned underground mines across the state.

One of the demanding jobs in the underground mines was manually shoveling the coal into small cars, which was then transported to the mine shaft itself. This was a tough, dirty, and dangerous occupation. On paydays, the miners would get paid in cash for the tonnage of coal they loaded, twenty-five cents for each car of coal filled. During World War II, technological improvements introduced electric driven coal loading machines into the mines. While this increased the output, it also eliminated many mining jobs.

To eliminate impurities (called slate), the mining company installed washers at the tipple to remove the slate from the coal before it was loaded into railroad cars. The slate would then be dumped in huge piles near the mines. Children often played on these slate piles, a dangerous place to play, and when they weren't playing, they were collecting leftover coal from the slate dump for the family's stove—their only source of heat. After many years of creating these piles, some over a hundred feet high and covering many acres, the dump would catch on fire from spontaneous combustion of the coal that was left with the slate. Abetted by high winds, the smoke would burn over the towns for several years, until the dump burned out. The remains of the burned-out slate were called "red dog" because of its red color, and was used to cover dirt roads and sides of paved roads for decades before environmental laws were passed to stop the pollution that resulted from rain runoff.

Due to water that seeped into the mines or to excess water that filled mines that had been emptied of coal, it became necessary periodically to pump water from the mines to keep them from flooding. This water was then discharged directly into nearby rivers and streams, which turned red from the polluting minerals. Mine pollution was a way of life then, and the people of western Pennsylvania learned to live with it.

In addition to negative functions of mining due to pollution, coal has also been called "black gold," for besides its value for heating purposes, coal, when heated, produces valuable byproducts. For example, eighty million tons of coal yields fifty million tons of coke, plus millions and even billions of dollars' worth of other products. One of these byproducts is a black gummy substance called coal tar; it is a favorite raw material for chemists, who are able to derive products from it such as dyes, perfumes, spot removers, drugs, fertilizers, and plastics. From this one compound chemists also derive saccharine, which is three hundred times sweeter than sugar; aspirin; disinfectants such as Lysol; coumarin, which is used in place of vanilla; a waterproofing substance used in concrete to keep water out of cellars; explosives such as dynamite and TNT; and poison gas.

All these benefits—and hazards—are in one piece of coal. One would never think so simply by looking at it. Although coal is readily available through mining, and is a rather inexpensive form of energy, it comes about through processes common in nature. However, it takes nature a long time to produce coal. As scientists tell us, coal is formed when dead plant matter submerged in swamp environments is subjected to the geological forces of heat and pressure over hundreds of millions of years.

As human beings have discovered, there are materials in coal that can be used for good or evil: drugs to cure the sick, explosives to be made into bombs to kill people in war, poison gas to spread destruction, and dyes of rainbow hue such as we have in our clothes. All of these byproducts can be used for good, but they can also be used to harm. And that, it seems, is not only true of all things in the world of nature; it is also true of us. As what is in coal can be used for good or evil, so the strength and abilities within each of us can be used for good or evil, good-will or vexation.

Georgia and Helen's Ancestral History (Paternal)

Georgia and Helen's great-grandmother Caroline Rakowitz (1888–1972), her surname a Germanized Slavic name, was born in what is today Lithuania (then part of the Russian Empire). In Lithuania she married John Paskutis (1886–1939), who came to Lithuania from a farm on the German border, his name in German meaning "a half-knight or a knight marries a commoner." They had one child, their daughter Helen, who was confirmed Roman Catholic at the age of thirteen in St. Petersburg. Her father, John Paskutis, left Lithuania in 1910 to save his brother, who would have been conscripted into the Russian army. Emigrating to southwestern Pennsylvania, he found mine work near McDonald, Pennsylvania, where he and his friends learned to wash away the coal dust at a local bar after work, intent on forgetting for a time the backbreaking labor and danger of the mine tunnels. Many of his coworkers were immigrants like himself.

Once settled, he sent for his wife Caroline, and shortly thereafter, their daughter Helen was born (1914–2014). Shortly thereafter, Caroline, accompanied by her infant daughter, returned to Lithuania to see her father, who was ill and who died shortly thereafter. Unable to return to her husband on account of World War I, her family lost their home in Kaunis, Lithuania, and Caroline and Helen they were forced to live with relatives, moving regularly due to the turmoil of the war.

Eventually, John saved enough money to send for his family. They returned to the United States in 1922 on board the Majestic, then the world's largest ocean liner and a sister ship of the Titanic, which had met its demise a decade earlier. Caroline, a classy, innovative lady, was unwilling to travel as a commoner, so she crossed the ocean in luxury—no third-class steerage for her!

While her husband worked in the mines, Caroline worked as a seamstress. She dressed fashionably, and loved ballroom dancing, high-fashion loves she passed on to her daughter Helen. As a hypochondriac, Caroline had trouble sleeping. To get better air circulation, she decided to sleep with her head at the feet of her bed and her feet at the head, especially in the summer, when company homes were like sweat boxes. She did not like fans, for they kept her awake at night. On one occasion, a thief scaled the trellis and broke into her second-floor bedroom. Finding Caroline in bed, he grabbed her ankles, thinking it was her head, trying to choke her. Fortunately, sleeping backward saved her life, for she was able to call out for help, forcing the burglar to run away, escaping through the open window.

When her daughter Helen came to the States in 1922, she hadn't yet learned to speak English. In high school, her accent prevented her from joining the debate team, but undaunted, she graduated as class valedictorian. She then went to nursing school, but was forced to quit due to a lack of funds. In the early 1930s, she met William Brown at a dance hall, where William was playing banjo with his band. As a member of a traveling band,

William had a car, and Helen jumped at the opportunity to meet him. Finding that his political views aligned with hers, she pursued a relationship that led to a civil marriage by a justice of the peace, followed by a church wedding. Despite their instant attraction, psychological, social, and religious differences led to a rocky road ahead, one they navigated together successfully for over forty years.

Fashionable like his wife, John Paskutis was a natty dresser, dressing up like a banker rather than a coal miner. He tended to be generous with his money, quick to lend it to his friends. At the age of fifty-seven he suffered a stroke, which left him with a limp and some degree of mental impairment. After an incomplete recovery from his illness, he went back to the mines, and even with a limp walked several miles to work. However, his mood darkened as the mine closed and he was left without the means to support himself and his family. These misfortunes occurred in the 1930s, an era that predated the use of public funds to provide for the aid of disabled workers, and he was too proud to accept the charity of menial work. One day he vanished, and search parties set out to locate him, fearing the worst, for when last seen he had been morose and dispirited.

It fell to his wife Caroline to find him, and she was never the same after she did so. She found him in the woods with an improvised noose around his neck. What a horrifying sight she must have beheld, finding his badly decomposed body. This was a difficult time for everyone, but none more difficult than for Caroline, who came to live with her daughter Helen and son-in-law William Brown and their four children.

Helen and Georgia trace their paternal ancestry back eleven generations to James Brown, who emigrated from Wellingsborough, Northamptonshire, England to the American province of West Jersey aboard the Kent in the summer of 1677, when 230 English Quakers arrived on Chygoes Island on the east bank of the Delaware River, settling in the newly founded riverfront community of Burlington in what today is a New Jersey suburb of Philadelphia. In 1676, the council of the province of West Jersey had purchase this land from the Lenape tribe of Indians. Over the next four years, five or ship ships followed, bringing 1,200 more immigrant to Burlington and other new towns in West Jersey. Many of these immigrants were Friends, as is attested by the freeholder census of 1699, which shows more than a third of the landowners in the proving of West Jersey were Quakers. They had emigrated from England prior to and as part of William

Penn's Settlers community in his colony of Pennsylvania, founded in 1681 to provide Quakers and fellow sectarians freedom of religion.

Accompanying James Brown on that 1677 voyage were William Clayton and Clayton's daughter Honour, whom James Brown married in 1679. Marriage records confirm James's trade as Weaver, and his residence at the time of his marriage as Upland, or Marcus Hook, on the Delaware River. From Marcus Hook James Brown Jr. (1681–c.1761) moved to Lancaster County in southeastern Pennsylvania, a region ideal for farming. In the early 1800s, David Brown (1803–1869) and his wife Rebecca Borland Brown relocated to western Pennsylvania, where he came into possession of a large tract of land that had once belonged to George Washington. In 1770, Washington had acquired 2,813 acres of land in western Pennsylvania (then likely part of what would become the state of Virginia) in what is now the town of Hickory in Mt. Pleasant Township in Washington County. In his will, David Brown deeded 107 acres to Matthew Borland Brown (1851–1925). As a successful farmer, Matthew also served as justice of the peace in Hickory. In an era early in the twentieth century when youth from small farms rarely went to college, Matthew raised a remarkable family with his wife Isabella (Bella) Russell Brown, producing a surgeon, a stockbroker, a columnist for a local newspaper, and another (John Brown) who became a state congressman, military officer under Theodore Roosevelt, a teacher and an apple grower.

Eventually his descendants purchased an apple business, running it for four generations. Existence of the orchard provided much of the impetus for the creation of an annual Apple Festival in Hickory, which draws visitors from Pittsburgh and surrounding communities during the last days of September. The founder of the business was John Edmund Brown (1976–1948), who often smelled of rotten eggs, an indication of the odor caused when spraying his trees with pesticides containing heavy doses of sulfur. The sprays he used are banned today, and health laws also require pasteurization of the main apple byproducts, cider and vinegar. There is little doubt that these now-banned sprays contributed to his death from lung cancer in 1948, at age seventy-two.

A product of the Victorian era and of Scots-Irish Presbyterianism, John was a stern patriarch who was ever gentle and kindly toward his offspring. He raised seven children, partly during the Great Depression, and though he produced no professional people, unlike his father Matthew, all of his children seemed to get along fairly well in life. His wife's surname was

Cook, one of whose relatives in England served as a personal bodyguard to Queen Victoria. John started his business in 1910, inheriting eight acres from his father Matthew, acreage that had once been owned by George Washington. Of the 107 acres that David Brown deeded to Matthew, eight ended up as John Brown's homestead. In 1910, John Brown created an orchard, adding a cider press in 1925.

Victorians like John Brown were formidable individuals. Following the Great Depression and the World War II, this generation became labeled "The Great Generation." As a young man, John Brown was an army officer and served during the Spanish-American War, a heritage honored at his funeral, done with full military honors. In addition to operating the apple orchard, John Brown taught school, was an electrician, and served as a representative of Washington County in the Pennsylvania State House. At his burial service, an elderly Black man sat in the front row at the gravesite, in honor of his work as a politician, when he spent many hours visiting potential black voters in their homes seeking their support. Coming from West Middletown, the elderly man had walked ten miles to pay his respects. Being an independent thinking person, John Brown managed to incur the wrath of David B. Lawrence, the political boss of the Democratic Party in the Pittsburgh area and the future governor of the state. Consequently, John's political career was short-lived, lasting but two years.

Despite his reputation as a stern Victorian Presbyterian, one of his grandsons once caught him at a weak moment, spotting him storing a bottle of whiskey inside a hollow apple tree. He kept it there because he knew that his wife would not permit him to keep and drink alcohol in their home. Victorian men tended to be patriarchal autocrats in their rural family farms, except when it came to everyday matters in the house, where Scotch-Irish matrons ruled with hands of iron. Similar stories circulate with respect to Matthew Brown, who also hid his booze from the eye of his sternly disapproving wife.

Life was not easy for John Brown's son William E. Brown (1904–1975), who to some extent was overshadowed by his dominant Victorian ancestors. No doubt being the second oldest male in an early twentieth-century farm family meant that he had to shoulder responsibilities that his younger siblings did not. Born with an artistic bent, for three years he attended night school studying art composition and drafting at what was then Carnegie Tech (now Carnegie Mellon University). Sadly, financial considerations forced him to abort his art education. Eventually his daughter Sally completed a master's degree in art and went on to teach the subject at a local elementary school. His granddaughter Georgia Lee took art classes at Washington & Jefferson College and displays her talent in watercolors and on murals.

William's first endeavor was to emulate his father by planting an apple orchard of about ten acres, and a patch of strawberries. For a time, while holding down an administrative job with the Pittsburgh Coal Company, he raised sheep and sold their wool. The mine job did not help his chronic asthma. Many nights he laid awake from intense coughing seizures, the only relief provided by powdery medication that he lit with a match and inhaled. In 1946 he took a bold risk in purchasing three greenhouses at a sale in Pittsburgh. That took courage, for in the spring of that year he had gained his first crop of chrysanthemums and carnations planted even before his greenhouses were erected, racing against a ticking clock before October frosts arrived. He did win that race, and he and his wife merged their talents to create a diversified business, which included the growing of flowers and vegetable plants, floral design, landscaping, and an evergreen nursey. Grandma Brown (William Brown's wife Helen Paskutis Brown) taught herself floral design, probably the most profitable part of the business, and Grandfather Brown handled everything else.

Life for this couple was definitely not easy. In addition to raising four children (Ron, born in 1935, John, in 1937, Tom, in 1939, and Sally, in 1951), both worked long hours, Matthew in his greenhouses and Helen in floral designs and sales. Much of their tension occurred at work. Often William could be seen rushing out late at night in frosty mid-winter in order to deal with malfunctions in the critical heating system for his greenhouses. Other pressures of the business included the requisite blooming of plants such as poinsettias during the Christmas season, and tulips planted in October had to bloom at Easter or else became unsaleable. Other pressures of the business included dealing with demanding customers and maintaining good help. Holidays like Mother's Day and Easter or large Italian funerals were particularly stressful for Helen, who often sat up late at night making corsages or funeral arrangements. There was one benefit from maintaining a greenhouse. Working in humid greenhouses and away from coal dust at the mine cured William's asthma.

A lover of great literature, Ron Brown (Georgia and Helen's father), eventually collected enough fine books to create one of the best personal libraries in the Pittsburgh area. His love of writing led to a legacy of an unpublished collection of poems and essays that he presented to each of his daughters. He wrote some of his essays to make his children aware of the accomplishments of their great-great grandfather Matthew Brown and their great-grandfather John Brown, as well as the sturdy blood of their great-grandfather John Pakutis, who toiled in the coal mines for twelve hours a day after walking several miles to work. He wants them to know about the high school exploits of their grandmother Helen Brown, which include her astounding feat of scoring seventy-six points in a single game on a championship team during the playoffs. Sadly, she never got the opportunity to follow up on what she achieved in high school by going to college. It must have been hard for her, gifted academically and athletically, to refuse college basketball scholarships because her parents could not afford even her campus incidental expenses.

Like his mother, Ron played basketball in high school, but unlike her, he was able to attend college, graduating with a business degree from Waynesburg College in Greene County, near the Pennsylvania-West Virginia border north of Morgantown, West Virginia. There he played varsity basketball for a while, including in a game against West Virginia University. After college he completed an MBA degree at Duquesne University in Pittsburgh before starting a career in finance and accounting in that city.

One day, while commuting by bus from Hickory to Pittsburgh, Ron met a tall, attractive lady named Georgia Ann Brinley. She had been married previously, but only briefly. Shy and lacking serious dating experience, Ron was immediately smitten. Georgia Ann was both good looking and intelligent. They were married in 1959 at Bethany United Presbyterian Church in Bridgeville, close to Georgia's home in Morgan, birthplace of their three children, twins Helen and Georgia (1961) and son Jimmy (1964–2008).

Many of Ron's essays speak of his love of nature, which led to an interest in landscaping and gardening, as evident in vast landscaping projects he has undertaken on properties he has owned. Other essays are about interesting people he has known, including his beloved high school English teacher Miss Elsie Cowden, who prepared him for success in required English grammar and composition classes in college, as well as about his love of birds, cats, and other delightful creatures. His essays also criticize and ridicule bad manners and vulgar social customs. Others demonstrate his love of historic sites and local shops such as hardware stores. Together, they display a heightened awe of the miracle of existence and the mystery of life. Currently, after two divorces, he lives with his third wife thirty miles north of Pittsburgh.

His hometown of Hickory, like many such small towns, has changed significantly, seemingly more a place of retirement now. As a youngster, the center of the village supported three neighborhood grocery stores, hardware and plumbing stores, and an antique shop, all of which are now gone. The old high school building has become a community center and playhouse. While some of the homes have been demolished or refurbished, including his grandparents' nursey and greenhouse, the old homestead still remains on Main Street (State Highway 50). Except for the popular annual apple festival, now waning, the town is no destination spot. When older folks look at villages like Hickory, they are reminded of Emma Goldman's comment regarding the city of Oakland, California, "There's no *There* there." Like other places in Washington County, including the county seat of Washington itself, which is arrayed in the splendor of newly planted trees and new brick walkways, college students and potential shoppers now vote with their cars against downtown renewal by fleeing to the outlying shopping malls, one mall now mostly vacated while others, losing established businesses, forever seem to be attracting new ones. Thomas Wolfe may have been right in asserting that we can't go home again, unless we realize that home is the human soul, and that renewal springs from within and not from without.

4

Georgia's Story

We all come to God in different ways. We encounter God and receive healing and guidance in unique and unexpected ways. Each of us has a story, and no two stories are alike. What I am about to relate is my life story, but more specifically, my spiritual journey.

A few years ago, my friend Lester tried to get me to quit smoking. I had overcome other addictions in the past, but had turned to food and cigarettes for comfort. Lester encouraged me to attend a service led by faith healer Billy Burke, a protégé of the well-known American evangelist Kathryn Kuhlman. Lester's persistence, together with my husband's support, resulted in a group of us attending a "World Outreach" healing service. Being naïve about healing services. I thought I could only ask for one healing, so I picked to quit smoking, something I had tried repeatedly and failed, for, like trying to stop diarrhea, quitting smoking involves more than willpower.

At that time I was experiencing many physical problems, including blood in my urine, COPD symptoms, weak knees, diabetes, high blood pressure, high cholesterol, and I was being tested for lung cancer. I believe Jesus led me to attend the healing service, for I found Pastor Billy Burke and his staff to be joyful and humble. When Pastor Burke asked, "Who has blood in the urine?" I went forward. Once I was up front, I began speaking privately with God, asking, "What have I done? I'm going to screw this up. Am I going to embarrass myself and everyone with me?" Then I saw a bright light, and immediately fell down. Jim told me later that I had been laughing on the floor. When I awoke, I got to my feet and cried. I had experienced grace! Full of joy, I felt a new surrender to the grace of the Holy Spirt, and I was amazed, for I had previously neglected this part of the Trinity.

At times I consider my experience as an exorcism. As many charismatics and evangelicals believe, evil in us may be due to demonic possession. Whether I had a demon or not, the change in me was sudden—and miraculous.

Since this healing, I have become a new person. The diabetes is gone, my COPD has cleared, I have new knees, I have no cancer, and have lost seventy pounds. In addition, I feel thirty years old! As a result, I follow Billy Burke World Outreach ministries and have learned to surrender completely to the triune God. Discipleship requires less effort now and produces far greater joy.

"Letting go and letting God"—that is the answer, for I have come to understand that discipleship involves total surrender to God. While helping others is beneficial emotionally to both givers and receivers, since such activity is known to release endorphins and to make everyone involved happier, I have come to learn the importance of caring for myself while putting others first. The secret of healthy compassion, I've discovered, starts with God's love.

• • •

As a child, I experienced three different family lifestyles, all in rural settings. The first three years of my life were spent with my mother, father, my twin sister Helen,[1] and for a short time with my younger brother Jimmy. Living in the town of Hickory, Pennsylvania, some twenty-five miles southwest of Pittsburgh, we grew up happy and healthy. My first memory is sitting on the right side of a baby stroller, looking to my left and seeing a baby. At that moment I realized the baby was not me. This was my first sense of selfhood.

Like many of us, I survived childhood, but only through the grace of God. Had it not been for Sissy and my grandparents, with whom Sissy and I lived during some of our early years, I would likely not have thrived. My mother was a devout Christian, so we regularly attended church at the Hickory United Presbyterian Church nearby.[2] Later in life, when my

1. Helen and I call one another "Sissy," so in this chapter, Sissy always refers to Helen, whereas in chapter 7, "Helen's story," Sissy refers to me.

2. The old church has succumbed to the wrecking ball and in 1969 the two Presbyterian churches in the village merged to form Hickory U.P. Church. This congregation left its parent denomination in 2012 to form Hickory United Evangelical Presbyterian Church. The cemetery of Mount Prospect Presbyterian Church remains, however, next

mother was dying, I asked her what the best day of her life had been. I expected her to say, "The day your sister and you were born," but I was pleasantly surprised with her answer, "The day I accepted Jesus." In 1963, when Sissy and I were about two and a half years old, the relative peace and security of our lives was turned upside down at the birth of our brother Jimmy, for my mother began suffering from postpartum depression.

As mothers know, the birth of a baby can start a variety of powerful emotions, from excitement and joy to fear and anxiety. But it can also result in something you might not expect—depression. Most new moms experience postpartum "baby blues" after childbirth, which commonly include mood swings, crying spells, anxiety and difficulty sleeping. Baby blues usually begin within the first two to three days after delivery and may last for up to two weeks. However, some new moms experience a more severe, long-lasting form of depression known as postpartum depression. Sometimes it's called peripartum depression because it can start during pregnancy and continue after childbirth. Rarely, an extreme mood disorder called postpartum psychosis also may develop after childbirth.

In the case of my mother, it was the severe, long-lasting form, and she began losing control not only of her children but also of herself. While I remember being afraid at times when it seemed like all control had left her, I also knew that she loved us fiercely and unconditionally. However, because she did not get immediate help, she experienced psychosis. Even then, she sent us to Sunday School and tried to meet our physical, emotional, and spiritual needs, but her inability to care for us, coupled with fear that she was unable to keep us safe or prevent us from running into the road, led to extreme punishments. Around that time, she became increasingly sick, and her growing mental illness led to further abuse. As our relatives recall, Sissy and I seemed wild and unruly. Like most children, we were highly imaginative and full of energy, and as twins, fully absorbed in each other. Individually independent, together we felt invincible, confident that two are braver than one.

When my parents' marriage failed and my mother and father separated, she was institutionalized and Sissy and I went to live with our paternal grandparents William and Helen Brown. They lived nearby, in a lovely rural setting about a mile from our previous home. While my brother Jimmy stayed with our dad and a hired caregiver, Sissy and I joined a larger

---

to the old churchyard, and the graves, including those of generations of Browns, remain well-tended.

household, for in addition to our grandparents and their two children, Sally (then in high school) and John (then away at college),[3] we lived with Great-Grandma Paskutis. For a while Grandpa Brown ran Brown's Fruit Farm, until he built a large greenhouse and became a florist. Grandma Brown, an effective businesswoman, ran Brown Flowers and Nursery. Watching them work and live a fulfilled lifestyle, we gained a strong work ethic.

Between our house and Highway 50 stood a split-rail fence built by Grandpa Brown, and behind our house was a large fenced pasture, where Sally kept Sham (meaning "sunlight" in Arabic), her palomino riding horse. She was an accomplished rider, competing regularly in costume classes and winning awards for costume design. Living with my relatives was like living in a nature conservancy. Flowers were everywhere, and Sissy and I were given a great deal of freedom. We often roamed at will, including playing in the nearby woods.

As a preschooler, I felt a strong bond with animals and all living creatures. Whenever an animal suffered or was abused by someone, I suffered as well. During this formative period, I shared everything with Sissy. We did everything together, and functioned as each other's half. Missing our mother, we often went into the woods together, looking for God. At this time I trusted God fully, viewing God as a living force in the universe, more like a spirit being than a human person.

The relationship I had with God, both then and now, is similar to the experience of bummer lambs, that is, of newborn lambs that for reasons of neglect or loss of the mother sheep, are known to be taken by shepherds into their homes, where they are bottle-fed, held, and kept warm by the family hearth. When the lamb is strong enough, it is taken back to the flock, but in the morning, when the shepherd calls the sheep, the first to run to the shepherd are the bummer lambs, who know the shepherd's voice. Does the shepherd love the bummer lambs more than the others? Not really, but they experienced the shepherd's love and care when they were vulnerable and broken, and that grace bonds the lambs to the shepherd for life.

I believe all people have a "bummer lamb" experience with God, whether it be when a parent dies, when divorce occurs, or through feelings of neglect, rejection, or abuse by others in our lives, and even later in life, by failed marriages, bad jobs, or rejection by friends or coworkers.

During the period when my mother was hospitalized and not present in our everyday lives, my father would come to visit us every night, when

3. Their third son, Tom, had already left home and was living on his own.

he read stories to us before putting us to bed. One of those stories was from a book by Rabelais about Gargantua and Pantagruel, giant characters with voracious appetites. The storybook was illustrated by Gustave Doré, the famous French painter, and he soon became my favorite artist, for his work fueled my artistic mind. Unfortunately, these stories also got me in trouble, for Sissy and I were now in first grade, and we delighted in retelling these stories in school.

I recall sitting in the front row and my sister in the back row. There were probably good reasons why our teacher had separated us. One day, however, she overheard Sissy telling our classmates the stories of Gargantua knocking on the door, and how it was so big that only its stomach and belly button were showing in the doorway. Observing the fearful response on the faces of the stunned children, the teacher asked me if a monster had visited my house.

"Is this true?" she asked. Fully expecting me to deny it. I paused and remember looking back at my sister, wondering what to say. However, I turned back to the teacher and answered, "Yes, it's true!"

For that response, we were sent home. Although this was the first such occurrence, getting sent home happened somewhat frequently. My dad must have been called, for he had to leave his accounting job in Pittsburgh to pick us up.

As I discovered later in life, our house had been visited by a monster. The monster of alcohol dependency and depression had visited our home, and would continue to haunt our family for many years.

Through my great grandmother's influence and my mother's faith, Sissy and I spent much of our time looking for God and praying for our mother every day. One day we found a discarded fruitcake in the firepit beyond the horse pasture, where my grandfather burned garbage. For some reason, Sissy and I equated the fruitcake with God. We returned to the greenhouse holding the fruitcake, announcing we had found God. Later on, when we learned that our grandfather had put "God" in the garbage, I felt violated. This event taught me to be gentle with the beliefs of others, knowing that while one person's beliefs might seem foolish or irrational to another, circumstances somehow make them sacred to the person who holds them.

Even though Sissy and I were happy in our grandparents' home, we longed for our mother, praying regularly for her return. One day Sissy and I were in the pasture, praying for her return, when I heard Sissy say, "There she is!"

We saw her appearance as an answer to prayer, and it strengthened our faith. However, due to shock therapy, she had changed. Sad and subdued, she was but a shell of herself. However, her drive to be with her family helped her overcome her mental illness, and she went on to overcome many obstacles, becoming a loving and successful single mother. Her return and recovery, which I saw as answered prayer, gifted me with the faith I have today.

Our mother had been institutionalized for a year for postpartum depression in Western State Psychiatric Institute and Clinic in 1963. Today psychiatrists estimate that between half and two-thirds of women experience some sort of postnatal depression shortly after childbirth. According to obstetrics texts, the nineteenth century, described as "the asylum era," is said to have had a "disastrous effect" on the management of women with puerperal psychoses, an effect that continued for much of the twentieth century. Called "puerperal insanity" or "puerperal mania," the disorder was devastating to those it struck, causing once calm women to physically and verbally strike out at both themselves and those around them. At its most severe, the disorder could result in infanticide or suicide. Even at its less extreme, a woman's behavior could seem disturbing and bizarre, leading to the neglect of her child, home, and her own body.

Electro-convulsive therapy ("ECT") was one method used to treat postpartum depression, along with frontal lobotomy. Both methods caused permanent damage to the brain. Many women never recovered, and were relinquished to perpetual institutionalization. However, in my mother's case, I believe her faithful drive to be with her children led to answered prayer, for after a year apart, mother and children were rejoined with God. As we read in Romans 5, "suffering produces endurance, and endurance produces character, and character produces hope, and hope does not disappoint us" (5:3–5).

Around the age of five, Sissy and I joined our mother in yet another move, this time to live with our maternal grandparents, Georgia and William Brinley, in the small mining town of Morgan, Pennsylvania, some ten miles away. The change in lifestyle was significant, for we went from abundance, self-assurance, and sufficiency to humility, financial limits, and humbler surroundings, a simpler lifestyle I now willfully adopt as my own. Grandma Brindley, who worked as a church secretary at Bethany United

Presbyterian Church in nearby Bridgeville, read to us from the Bible every night, and this habit increased my faith and deepened my love of scripture. Our religious community was enlarged by participating in the worship and life of two congregations, my grandmother's larger church and the much smaller but more intimate church setting provided by my mother, who attended Gladden United Presbyterian Church.

In Morgan, Sissy and I were placed in different classes, and my sister and I began going our own way. She had more friends than I did, and we ran in different social circles. As a child, I naturally associated with African-American boys and girls, and considered many of them friends. However, I also picked up prejudiced social and racial views from the dominant white culture, and I remember calling Black children insulting names and picking fights with them. In retrospect, I behaved like a bully, not because of something in them or about them, but because of something in me. By seventh and eighth grade, having reached my height of 5 feet 11½ inches and a weight of around 150 pounds, I could dominate others physically, yet I still felt vulnerable and fearful, and for a while I tried taking my insecurity out on others. Gradually, however, as I got to know and spend time with some of these children, friendship overcame prejudice.

As sixth grade came to a close and as students anticipated moving to junior high, we heard that while there we would be divided into four distinct groups. "Make sure you avoid Section 4," we were told, "because that's where stupid students are placed."

The following term, on the first day of class, Sissy and I were separated yet again; I was placed in Section 4, and Sissy in Section 3. In Section 4, I was surrounded by troublemakers and academically marginal students. Many of them seemed sad and depressed, resigned to boredom, futility, and unhappiness. I also found myself studying with older boys who had been held back due to failure, and I feared I had been given a label that I was not smart. Having begun grade school a year earlier than most other students, I was still only twelve years old, yet beside me sat a sixteen-year-old girl who looked like a fully grown woman. I wasn't yet ready for her level of conversation, which included telling me that her aunt was in jail, for I had never known anyone whose relative was in jail. She also let me know that she had slept with the uncle of the children for whom she babysat.

Because I was tall, strong, and athletic, people might have presumed I was unintelligent, which I was not. In retrospect, I may have been placed in Section 4 because of my bullying behavior. Being in Section 4 humbled me, and caused me to abandon my bullying behavior. Thus, when I got to high school, when students were no longer classified arbitrarily, I was determined to nullify my previous classification through academic achievement. And that proved successful, for during my senior year I became an honor student, graduating 13th in a class of 106. In addition to my required curriculum, I also took art electives. I had always been interested in art, ever since living with Grandma Brown and my aunt Sally, whose love of art and design influenced me greatly. At Christmas, they often gave Sissy and me coloring and painting kits. That interest continued in high school, when I was elected president of the art club, and later in college and in my professional life.

During high school and later, in college, my sister and I mixed with different social groups. Sissy's friends were more popular and numerous, and mine quirkier. In high school I was a varsity athlete, running distance events on the track team and a starting player on the girls' basketball team, where I set the school record with 34 points in a game. During my junior year, I visited Washington & Jefferson College (W&J), where I met Coach Staton, the college women's basketball and volleyball coach, and she persuaded my high school coach to move me from the guard position to center forward.

After graduating from high school in 1978, I immediately enrolled at W&J, where I excelled in basketball, starting all four years. At this time, my sister and I roomed together, and though we took different classes and sought different majors, we were both on the same basketball team. In addition to playing on a championship basketball team, I also played volleyball. I had only played volleyball one year in high school, but from basketball and also valuing my height and size, Coach Staton recognized my potential as a volleyball player, and I must have been a quick learner, for in addition to receiving the MVP award as a junior, I was also honored with "All Conference" status my sophomore, junior, and senior years.

The year 1969 was difficult for my family. Sissy and I were only eight years old when my father, now divorced from my mother, remarried and relocated to a community north of Pittsburgh. That year was also traumatic in that my grandfather William Brinley died of alcoholism. Following the mine closure and his retirement, his personal life had deteriorated greatly, and he began drinking a case of beer and a fifth of whiskey daily. During that time he also lost a leg due to gangrene, as we often saw him sad and depressed and confined to a wheelchair. Though he was a generous man, helping people who had been laid off or who were experiencing financial difficulties, he regularly received threatening calls from disenfranchised workers and local agitators. There is no question that he feared for himself and his family, and that underlying fear surely contributed to his alcoholism.

Naturally, this fear spread to his family members, for it left me with a fear of death, for myself and those around me. For three months I worried and fretted, sharing my fears regularly with my grandmother. Lacking assurance and comfort, I decided to pray, and after doing so, I noticed a notable change of heart, for my fear of death disappeared for good. The suffering of that period, coupled with earnest prayer, yielded the kind of faith Jeremiah discovered in suffering: "I will turn their mourning into joy, I will comfort them, and give them gladness for sorrow" (31:13).

Alcohol had long been an issue in our house. My grandfather Brinley had died from it, and my mother was greatly afflicted by it as well, until she overcame her alcoholism when I was a teenager. Though my mother was an alcoholic and my father was a maintenance drinker (one who drinks daily, yet remains functional), we had been raised not to drink. My father was often away from home, working long hours, and he missed out on being with his family. Yet when he did spend time with us, he was funny and a source of delight. Often, when grandparents raise their grandchildren, fathers and mothers become demoted to brother and sister roles, and that's what happened with us. Though I enjoyed being with them, my parents seemed more like siblings than guardians and caregivers.

At the age of sixteen, I drank my first beer, and I was instantly addicted, for I found alcohol did for me what neither others nor I could do for myself. Since the age of twelve, I had lived with many fears—fear of poverty, of misery, of reputation—but particularly of mental illness. My mother had been diagnosed as schizophrenic, and I feared I too would be labeled abnormal or socially unfit. At this time, my mom and I visited Carol Yablonski (niece of murdered UMWA union leader Jock Yablonski), then institutionalized at Woodville State Hospital, in part for her own protection, for she was kept separated from the other residents, and there was no question in our minds that she was quite sane. She was working on a book about her uncle's assassination, and my mother and I visited her weekly, providing her with background information for her book. I became convinced her anxieties came from the trauma her family had experienced. These visits were pivotal for me, for they helped me realize that peoples' actions can make others crazy. I became aware that mental illness need not be congenital, but that it could be caused by various factors, many of them external to the individual.

My mother's actions also contributed to my fears and insecurities. My mother often went out of her way to befriend needy people, but many of them were peculiar and even deviant. Some of them became my friends as well, and when I introduced them to "normal" or more ordinary individuals, they were not well received. Association with peculiar people made me apprehensive, because I didn't want to be socially isolated or unfit. When I was introduced to the Presidential Physical Fitness Award challenge in junior and senior high school, I participated immediately, not only because it required physical accomplishments, but also because it stressed mental fitness. While physical fitness came naturally to me, mental fitness was something I craved.

My first alcoholic drink gave me immediate relief, for my insecurities and fears instantly subsided. My parents and grandparents had taught me not to drink, but at that point I felt betrayed by their prohibitions. As my defenses crumbled, I changed my mind about not drinking. Drinking was fun and empowering, and I began believing the illusion that I could control my drink. Previously, I had decided I would never drink, but now, for the first time ever, I felt I was in control, and I succumbed to the lie that addiction is a weakness anyone can master. I had embarked on a treacherous path.

I took my second drink when I visited W&J as a prospective student. I was with strangers, and rather than maturing my social skills, alcohol helped loosen my social inhibitions. Drinking became a panacea, for it took my fears away, helped me relax and fit in, and made me feel everything would be okay. On that occasion, I drank until I threw up, and yet I still believed I could control my intake. I chased the next drink and then another, oblivious to its tantalizing power. The path of least resistance beckoned, and I became a frequent traveler.

After drinking, I remember crying, possibly from guilt, but more deeply because when I drank, I felt separated from God. Soon alcohol replaced God in my life. My drinking spree continued for sixteen years, and it only ended when I became reconciled to God, when I actively yielded control of my life to God.

After graduating from high school, I met a boy at work and we bonded immediately. I began dating him during my freshman year, when he began visiting me at school. I liked him, but I knew I couldn't marry him, because he was an alcoholic. I knew I was an alcoholic, but I didn't accept responsibility. As I know now, an alcoholic is not simply one who drinks often or irresponsibly, but one who drinks for effect. The first time I drank, my entire perspective changed. In college, there was no question I was an alcoholic. I drank with my boyfriend, I drank with my athletic teammates, and I drank with my friends. However, I wasn't a social drinker; I was an alcoholic, for I drank for effect.

In my senior year at W&J, having turned twenty-one years of age and legally an adult no longer dependent on my parents for support, I took a job working for the college. My stepmother had decided to attend college, and due to additional financial costs, my father decided I should earn my own spending money. Having reached another milestone in my life, I became increasingly stressed, both academically and personally. Lacking focus and concentration, I failed Spanish. Having no plans to further my education by applying to graduate school, I had begun skipping classes, trusting I could catch up at exam time and get a passing grade. That might have worked in some classes, but not with a foreign language, which requires daily participation. For some reason, I attended my World Religions class faithfully, for I respected the subject matter, which impacted me personally, and I felt a bond with my professor, Dr. Vande Kappelle (whom students called "Dr. Van"), and I didn't wish to disappoint him. Being strong in mathematics, I also passed my accounting class. However, I didn't show up for my other final exams, and failed those classes as well.

In addition to my poor academic performance, I was in a relationship with a guy. This was not my first such experience in college, but I noticed that when the guys seemed interested in a more committed relationship, I wasn't. I just wanted a dating relationship. I looked forward to getting married eventually, but not yet. No one in my family encouraged marriage, and that included my mother and both my grandmothers. I remember my grandmother Brown saying, "You don't need to get married; you were born a twin!"

Aware that I was experiencing mild depression, my boyfriend and I simply grew apart. I was still obsessed that I might be schizophrenic. I felt I was not hearing or seeing properly, and that I was somehow unprepared or unfit for normal adulthood. I began labeling myself "schizophrenic": when I failed Spanish, it was because I was schizophrenic; when I dropped out of basketball my senior year, I felt it was caused by schizophrenia; and at the end of my senior year, when I failed to graduate, I simply walked away. Why not? I was schizophrenic!

As a college student, particularly as I faced graduation, my mental state was "feral," a term often used of wild or undomesticated animals. I feared authority, and I had trouble opening up or trusting others. I couldn't trust someone enough to get married, and certainly not enough to become pregnant. Thus, whenever opportunities arose to pursue marriage, I declined them. After all, that wasn't the reason I dated, for I wasn't ready for a committed relationship. Besides, I knew from experience that I couldn't trust educated men. My dad had served as an example. He had been well educated, and he had cheated on my mom. His behavior gave me cause for suspicion and even for resentment. In my case, loyalty became essential for any long-lasting relationship. Incidentally, both Sissy and I have trust issues, and I believe it is the reason why we both married working-class men.

Looking back, distrust and suspicion was part of a pattern for me. In high school, I had been shy, not because I was born that way but because I hadn't wanted to be viewed as crazy or insane. I shared the same name as my mother—Georgia—and when I was around twelve years old, people would call our home asking for "Georgia." Many of these were crank calls, often containing sexual slurs and innuendos. My mom had become sexually promiscuous, and I knew these calls were meant for her, but I feared I too would be labeled "abnormal."

Eventually, I felt I could conquer my fears with alcohol, but drinking only made things worse. I needed to grow up, and growing up meant acquiring responsible social skills. Later on, as a sober adult, I learned to challenge myself, overcoming my fears and isolation by living empathetically, loving God by loving myself and others simultaneously.

I cannot speak about myself or even understand myself without speaking of my mother, for our relationship was both complex and impactful on my mindset and behavior. The expression "you owe me" sticks with me. I heard it from my coaches but also from my mother, and I realize I have bought into obligation. As I was completing my college education, I feared getting a job, for I felt inadequate. Knowing my mother and grandmother needed care and expected me to be their caregiver, I used this concern as an excuse. When, in my junior year, my mother gave my sister and me a new pair of shoes, the message was clear. My sister's loafers were fashionable, whereas my gift was a white pair of nursing shoes. This validated my suspicion. I was to be her nurse, her personal caregiver!

I was raised in an old-fashioned family. Like in generations past, my mother and grandmother Brindley pressured Sissy and me to care for them in their old age, as had been done in past generations. This expectation, coupled with my fears and insecurities, provided me with a social hiding place. Having been raised by my grandmother, now a widow, and having a mother who needed adult care and supervision, I felt uniquely responsible for them. My peers seemed to face different circumstances, but at times people told me they wished a relationship with their mother and grandmother like mine, and one even added how nice it was to be needed. I began to consider myself special, anointed by God to become a caregiver.

Despite her caring nature, my mother drank alcoholically, and this addiction influenced both her thoughts and actions significantly. Around the time I finished college, she encouraged me to file a federal disability claim, so the government would take care of us. That had worked for her, and she wanted me to seek welfare and learn "to work the system." She had cared for her mother that way, and having undergone shock treatments, she did not always think clearly or responsibly. Like her, I too was motivated by deep-rooted fears and insecurities, conditions exacerbated by alcoholism.

Although my mother didn't particularly like children, she always helped people in need, inviting needy individuals to our home, many of them addicts. Living promiscuously, some of her companions tried to proposition Sissy and me. On one such occasion, we locked one of her lovers in the basement. My mother eventually sought help for her alcoholically induced behavior, and she became sober in 2003, remaining sober until her death in 2015.

When Sissy and I finished college, we returned home to live with my mother and grandmother. My grandmother was now eighty years old and she and my mother needed care and security. Hearing stories from a friend who worked in nursing homes about how elderly patients sometimes get raped while living there certainly put us all on guard, and the last thing Sissy and I wanted was for our grandmother and mother to end up in such circumstances.

After college, my sister and I worked for a housecleaning service. That continued from 1982 until 1988. During that time, I attended an art institute, after which I worked as a commercial artist (1984–1986). In 1988 Sissy and I contacted some of our drinking friends and we started a cleaning business called Capital Cleaning Services. Soon thereafter my sister met and married Ray Morrow and moved in with him. She continued working with me until her son Ray was born, and the burden of the business fell on me. In 1989 Sissy moved to California with her husband and son, at which time I moved to live with my brother Jim, and my sister-in-law Sandy and her son Fidel, who joined me in my cleaning service. Working with me became a stepping stone for many of my workers, who learned discipline and accountability and developed a stronger work ethic while under my supervision.

In 1993, I stopped drinking, and by the grace of God I remained sober for the rest of my life. For ten years, ever since W&J, I had tried to quit drinking. I tried to get help, but only half-heartedly and sporadically. Over the years, my grandfather had attended behavioral self-help therapy meetings for recovering alcoholics, and when my mother began attending, I occasionally joined her, but I wasn't seriously committed to the process. I continued to believe the lie that I was in charge, and that I could stop drinking on my own.

In 1993, my self-deception ended when I committed my life to Christ. Through the help of a Catholic priest, I experienced true repentance, meaning confessing of wrongdoing, accepting responsibility for my actions, and committing to restitution and change, and it was then that I came to understand the saving work of Jesus. Significantly, the priest's role was passive rather than active, for he functioned as an intermediary, and that experience initiated my longing for a relationship with Jesus, a relationship I had not known to be possible. Experiencing God's grace, I felt connected to Christ, and that relationship became spiritual bedrock.

I had attended church occasionally, but I returned to Gladden Presbyterian Church, where I worshipped faithfully as a child. Submitting to the lordship of Christ and to divine authority, I also acquired a love for scripture, and it became my goal to read the Bible from cover to cover, something I have now done eight times. On one occasion, I was led to draw about forty illustrations of scenes in the Bible, including my favorite of Jacob wrestling with God. Relying on Jesus and on scripture made life much easier to navigate, and I found myself obsessed with spirituality.

Two years later, while still running Capital Cleaning, I began working in a nursing home. I thought I might benefit from having a boss, so when I saw an add in the newspaper advertising a job as activities and recreation director in a nursing home, I jumped at the opportunity. At that time, a friend of my mother named Alice was an employee in my cleaning business, and she encouraged me to apply. When I was called in for an interview, I was hopeful of getting the job. When I was offered the job, Alice told me I was lucky to get the job over many other applicants. I guess she wanted to encourage me, for I fell for her line. It was only later, after accepting the job, that I learned I had been the only applicant.

Now I was working two jobs, and I was doing so twelve hours a day, seven days a week. No longer an alcoholic, I had become a workaholic. Having relinquished alcohol, I discovered an endless set of substitute compulsions. I wanted to buy a house, get a credit card, take others to eat, meet new people, and find a husband. I felt ready for marriage; all I needed was a suitor. I had always wanted to get married, but I feared making a poor choice, and I certainly didn't want to marry an alcoholic. Experience had taught me that such a marriage would not work for me.

My workaholic pattern lasted for seven years. During that period, I kept my cleaning business while taking a second job as activities program assistant in a nursing home. I followed my boss, Terry Eger, from one nursing home to another. Terry, a tall, elegant, athletic lady, had been an All-American basketball player at a major Ohio university, and she had known my college coach as well, so I felt comfortable under her supervision. There was no question that God had brought her into my life, for she became a close friend and mentor. Eventually she played a major role in my marriage, supporting me when I met and married Jim Metsger in 2000. The residents of my new nursing home became like family to me then, even helping me pick out a wedding dress.

Georgia's Personality and Spirituality Profile

Georgia's MBTI results are ENFJ. Described as Protagonist, she is a person with Extraverted, Intuitive, Feeling, and Judging personality traits. These warm, forthright types love helping others, and they tend to have strong ideas and values. They back their perspective with the creative energy to achieve their goals. ENFJs feel called to serve a greater purpose in life. Thoughtful and idealistic, these personality types strive to have a positive impact on other people and the world around them. They rarely shy away from an opportunity to do the right thing, even when doing so is far from easy.

Protagonists are born leaders; their passion and charisma allow them to inspire others not just in their careers but in every arena of their lives, including their relationships. Few things bring Protagonists a deeper sense of joy and fulfillment than guiding friends and loved ones to grow into their best selves. Protagonists tend to be vocal about their values, including authenticity and altruism. When something strikes them as unjust or wrong, they speak up. These personality types have an uncanny ability to pick up on people's underlying motivations and beliefs. Their flashes of insight can make them incredibly persuasive and inspiring communicators.

ENFJ's secret weapon is their purity of intent. Generally speaking, they are motivated by a sincere wish to do what is right rather than a desire to manipulate or have power over others. Even when they disagree with someone, they search for common ground. When Protagonists care about someone, they want to help solve that person's problems—sometimes at any cost. There's a reason that these individuals have a reputation for helping others improve their lives, for people often seek Protagonists' assistance and advice. However, getting involved in other people's problems isn't always a recipe for success. Protagonists tend to have a clear vision of what people can or should do in order to better themselves, but not everyone is ready to make those changes. If Protagonists push too hard, their loved ones may feel resentful or unfairly judged. And while this personality type is known for being insightful, even the wisest Protagonists may sometimes misread a situation or unwittingly give bad advice.

People with this personality type are devoted altruists, ready to take on suffering and adversity in order to stand up for the people and ideas that they believe in. This strength of conviction bolsters their innate leadership skills, particularly their ability to guide people to work together in the service of the greater good. Their greatest gift is actually leading by example, for in their everyday lives, they handle seemingly unreal situations with compassion, dedication, and care. For these personalities, even the smallest daily choices and actions can become opportunities for exemplary behavior.

Passionate, reliable, altruistic, and charismatic, Protagonists also have strong opinions, but they are far from closed-minded. They recognize the importance of allowing others to express themselves fully. Despite clear, attractive strengths and virtues, Protagonists can be overly idealistic, overly empathetic, and unrealistic. While Protagonists tend to put pressure on themselves to right every wrong that they encounter, they often spread themselves too thin, and consequently are in need of help themselves. While compassion is among this personality type's greatest strengths, Protagonists have a tendency to take on other people's problems as their own, a habit that can leave them emotionally and physically drained.

When it comes to romantic relationships, Protagonists can be intense when it comes to matters of the heart. People with this personality type rarely settle for anything that falls short of their ideals, and their romantic relationships are no exception. Although these personalities may come across as outgoing and even a bit flirtatious, few Protagonists are satisfied by fleeting attractions. Their standards are high, and they know it. When Protagonists fall for someone, they tend to fall hard, so much so that they often find themselves making the first move. That said, because Protagonists often make the first move, they may encounter their share of rejection as they search for a kindred spirit.

Even on a first date, these personalities may steer the conversation toward weightier topics. This quality often affects what television shows they watch, and what social media they follow. Some Protagonists carry this quality too far, taking on their partner's goals as their own. This can be problematic, in that they may end up neglecting their own self-care, hobbies, and friendships. They may also be at risk of pushing their partner to change his or her life in ways that they simply aren't ready for. For this reason, their partner may become insecure, fearing that they aren't good enough as they are, or they may become resentful of the implication that they need to change. Either way, Protagonists must learn to encourage their partner to grow without pushing too hard.

Protagonists take dating and relationships seriously. Even in the earliest days of a relationship, Protagonists tend to focus on long-term potential, and as the relationship matures, they want to do what it takes to bring that potential to fruition. This can be grand for the partner, for Protagonists care about pleasing their partner, and their sensitivity helps them tune in to their partner's shifting moods and desires. As long as they don't lose track of their own needs, people with this personality type can enjoy incredibly rewarding relationships that are founded on trust, mutual support, and honesty, and, of course, love.

Connecting with other people makes Protagonists feel alive and purposeful. It is no surprise, then, that they put sincere, dedicated effort into staying close with their friends. For these personalities, friendships are a key component of a life well lived. Few personality types can match Protagonists' sincere desire to get to know people of diverse beliefs, culture, and lifestyles. Most Protagonists are fascinated by other worldviews, even those with which they wholeheartedly disagree. Encountering a wealth of perspectives is what keeps life interesting for this type.

This curiosity and openness might help explain Georgia's spirituality, which might be described as holistic, for there is a part of her spiritual perspective that is deeply evangelical, conservative, and charismatic, and another part that is deeply progressive, ecumenical, and liberating. It is almost as if she is able to live fully in first and second half of life settings simultaneously.

That said, most Protagonists find it difficult to respect anyone who takes shortcuts, disrespects others, or refuses to challenge the status quo. Instead, they find it easiest to connect with people who share their core ideals, particularly their commitment to doing the right thing and leaving the world better than they found it.

Protagonists can be among the best friends anyone could wish for. Kindhearted and trustworthy, people with this personality type dedicate incredible amounts of energy and attention to their friendships. They want their friends to feel not merely validated but supported, not merely heard but understood. Nothing makes Protagonists happier than seeing the people they care about doing well, and few things could stop them from trying to help make that happy.

Speaking as her friend, I found all of the above-mentioned qualities to describe Georgia quite precisely. As she and Jim demonstrate, the most enduring friendships are based not only on mutual growth but also on acceptance, compassion, and genuine respect.

Georgia's personality typology on the Enneagram is supportive and compatible with her MBTI preferences, for on the Enneagram she types as a Type Two (dominant) with a Three "wing" (auxiliary). Type Two are called Helpers or Givers. Twos are empathetic, sincere, and warm-hearted. Their primary virtue is *Humility*. They are friendly, generous, and self-sacrificing, but they can also be sentimental, flattering, and people-pleasing. They are driven to be close to others, and they often do things for others in order to be needed. They typically have problems taking care of themselves and acknowledging their own needs. Their primary Passion is *Pride*, better described as Vainglory—pride in their own virtue. At their best, healthy Twos are unselfish and altruistic and have unconditional love for themselves and others.

As a personality having a Type Three "wing," Georgia is also an Achiever or Performer. Threes are self-assured, attractive, and charming. Their primary virtue is *Truthfulness*. Ambitious, competent, and energetic, they can also be status-conscious and highly driven for personal advancement. Threes are often concerned about their image and what others think of them. They typically have problems with workaholism and competitiveness. Their primary passion is *Vanity* or deceit, putting effort into developing their ego instead of their true nature. At their best, healthy Threes are self-accepting, authentic, and everything they seem to be—role models who inspire others.

As an ENFJ, Georgia's spirituality type is "NF." As noted in chapter 2,

> NFs are characterized by a *questing spirituality*. NF youth like to please the adults and peers in their lives. They can be easily crushed by disapproval or even indifference. They need regular affirmation from parents and teachers if their self-esteem and self-image are not to suffer. Because they see possibilities in the future (N) and like to gain approval from others, they often will prepare for careers and causes in response to adult mentors in their lives. NF youth are exceedingly idealistic. Their idealism is often unpredictable; some young men may overcompensate for their F by expressing their idealism in hostile ways. They are strongly represented among protestors for social issues. NF adults are enthusiastic and insightful, recognizing the personal needs of others. Idealists by nature, they always see a way to make life better. They have an ability to draw people into a discussion and to facilitate consensus-building for social harmony and good. NFs on a healthy track will regularly draw others toward their own best selves. The Intuitive proclivity for symbol and metaphor, combining with global vision for the well-being of the world, makes NFs inspired communicators of the ideal. Future-oriented and attuned to the big picture of life as a whole, NFs tend to focus more on possibilities than on concrete situations at hand. Their N nature is balanced, however, by their F side, which keeps them in touch with reality and keeps their utopian bent in check. Flexible and open to change, NFs see life as continual self-creating process, a quest toward selfhood. Their malleable natures exist to be formed and re-formed in ever more exquisite patterns of self-actualization. NFs seek increasing meaning and spiritual purpose in life.

Combining Urban Holmes' Spirituality Wheel and John Westerhoff's approach, as an "F," Georgia's spiritual typological preference is Type II: affective-kataphatic or charismatic (a heartfelt, intuitive spirituality). This type, a sensate, heartfelt approach to spirituality, aims to achieve holiness of life through personal renewal.

5

Jim's Story

When I was six years old, my friend Bob and I were playing in a vacant lot beside my house. Unaware, Bob stepped into a yellow jacket nest in the ground and was stung by a swarm of bees. Panic stricken and afraid for my life, I ran away, calling for my mom. When she came and saw how badly Bob had been stung, she took him to the hospital. He must have been highly allergic to bee stings, for he did not survive the attack, dying in the hospital. My immediate response was to question, "Why would God allow this to happen?" As most children, I had a sincere faith, but it was quite naïve. In addition, I feared for my life, aware that I too might get stung and die. That was my first encounter with death, but it would not be my last.

• • •

I was born in 1946 in Connellsville, Pennsylvania at a very young age. While my surname Metsger means "butcher" or "grocer" in German, I'm glad I wasn't born in Germany, because I can't speak German. As the story goes, my father called my grandmother and told her my mom said, "It's another boy." My parents already had three boys (Larry, Jack, and Bob) and it seemed I was a disappointment. However, fifteen minutes later my dad called my grandma again and this time excitedly announced, "It's a girl!" That's right, I had a twin sister. We were named James and Joan, not by our parents, but by the doctor. Hearing later in life that I had been somewhat of a disappointment to my parents at birth made me resentful.

My parents, like those of many others I know, were down-to-earth, matter-of-fact, practical people. Like many other blue-collar families, they kept a genealogical record, but didn't spend much time passing down anecdotal stories. I was taught, however, that in 1682, my paternal ancestor Christian Metzger came from Germany to America, where he settled in what became Lehigh, Pennsylvania, earning a living as a millworker. My paternal grandfather was a grocer, who ran his own store until he went bankrupt during the Great Depression. My maternal ancestors, however, were English, and my earliest memory of that side of the family goes back to my maternal grandfather Edward B. King, who worked in the steel mills of western Pennsylvania. My mother (Ruth Katherine King, 1911–1990) was a registered nurse but a stay-at-home mom. My father (Lawrence Kiester Metsger, 1912–1989) was a fireman on the Pennsylvania railroad. Mom would pack his grip and off he went, traveling from Connellsville to Conway, about two hours by train each way. Though we were well fed and had a roof over our heads, we grew up in poverty, and we managed to keep most of it. At the age of seven we moved from Connellsville to Wilkinsburg and that led to my second resentment: I had left all my friends. My first address was 1201½ Chestnut Street. My mom taught us to remember our address using symbols. When she said "Chest" she touched her chest, and when she said "nut" she touched her head. We practiced over and over, saying "chest" by touching our chest and "nut" touching our head, until we got it.

I was good with images and symbols, so when my parents took us to church on Sundays, I immediately grasped the concept of God. When I entered fifth grade, I inherited a paper route from my brother Bob. For six years. I got up at 5 a.m. to deliver papers to fifty-five customers. However, when it came time for my boss to pick up the money for the papers, I was always short, and my dad would always make up the difference. It took a while before I discovered that my brother Jack was stealing from me.

Jack was mischievous, and quite a character. On one occasion, he got a job digging graves. One Saturday he took me with him to the cemetery. After removing the sod, we began digging a hole six feet deep, six feet long, and three feet wide, using only a pick and two shovels. Shortly after starting, he told me he had forgotten something but would be right back. After giving me something to drink, he left, and never came back. Nine hours later it began getting dark and I heard a swishing sound nearby, and then something hit me in the leg. Scared out of my wits, I jumped out of the hole and ran all the way home, a distance of about three miles. Out of curiosity, I returned the next morning to locate the source of my terror, only to find a solitary rabbit still in the pit. Jack, on the other hand, had spent a relaxing day with his girlfriend, and that's the last time I helped him dig graves.

Later on, Jack worked in a gas station fixing cars. One day he decided to rob the station. He prepared by changing his clothes and by putting a stocking over his face, but when he went to rob his station, he forgot to take off his work shirt—the one with his name on it. Needless to say, he got caught, and was sent to juvenile detention to work off his sentence. One day he decided to escape, but when he got home, the police were waiting for him. He finally got his life together, and after high school he joined the army for four years, then enlisted in the navy for another four years. He eventually became a cross-country truck driver, and then a streetcar driver in Boston. In 1996, while only 61 years of age, he died of a stomach aneurism, the same malady from which both of my parents had died.

I was a straight A student from kindergarten until sixth grade. At the age of twelve I was raped by my uncle and I thought God had turned his back on me. I got depressed and my grades tumbled, leading to failing seventh grade. Around that time my dad brought home a jug of homemade wine from work and placed it on a shelf in the basement. After hearing of being raped by my uncle, my older brother Moose (Bob) told me to get a glass and join him in the basement. Moose was my hero. As mentor, he helped shape my values and my sports life, teaching me how to handle problems and how to live. We talked about how I would become a Pittsburgh Steeler when I grew up.

In the basement, Moose opened Dad's jug of wine and poured us a glass. Taking a swig, he spit it out, claiming it tasted terrible. When I took a drink, I liked it. In addition to making me feel warm and fuzzy, it gave me a sense of pride. I felt grownup and more importantly, powerful. After that drink I was never raped again. I now was able to stand up to my uncle and felt fearless. I had been abused, but I wouldn't become an abuser.

Over time, I went back to the basement, drinking from that jug until it was empty. When I realized the bottle was empty, I panicked, knowing my dad would find out, so I filled the bottle up with water. However, even with compromised taste buds, it didn't taste right. I went back upstairs and found some food coloring from my mom's pantry, but my alcoholic brain told me that my dad would know the difference. Further panicked, I took a hammer and broke the jug over the steps. When my dad came home, I was still cleaning up the mess. Seeing him watch me clean up the broken glass, I explained that running down the steps had caused the bottle to fall from the shelf. I was only twelve years old, yet I was a full-blown alcoholic and a chronic liar.

When my dad told me everything was okay, I grew confident in my own lies, thinking I had just pulled something over on my dad. The thought that I could get away with anything followed me throughout my drinking career. Only later, four years after I had stopped drinking, my dad told me he had known the truth all along. I guess the only person I had fooled was myself. I was in seventh grade when those episodes took place, and it was a rough year. I was unable to study or concentrate at school, and ended up flunking that grade. Thankfully, after that I was able to get by with my grades, eventually graduating from high school.

Though I had below average grades in high school, I had remarkable speed and was gifted athletically. In addition to running track, I played baseball, football, and basketball, and was on the wrestling team. In football I played as an end on offense and as a middle linebacker on defense. I began envisioning a career with the Pittsburgh Steelers, but those dreams came to an abrupt end in my senior year when an opposing player stepped on my calf with his sharp cleats, leaving a deep puncture. I was on crutches for a month until my coach told me if I didn't suit up and start practicing I would be off the team. Suffering with chronic pain, I refused, and was kicked off the team. This wasn't the first time the coach had kicked a Metzger off the team. He had coached my brother Larry and for some reason he too had been kicked off the team.

In 1965, our nation was at war with North Vietnam, and I was a patriot. That summer after my graduation a recruiter from the Navy came to my house and arranged for me to go into the Navy to train in radio communication. He had checked my Boy Scout record and saw that I had some training in communications. I signed up on a 120-day delayed entry plan, and was under no delusion as to where I would end up.

Why did I enlist in the military to fight a war far away in a complex cause I hardly understood? While there are many causes, some subliminal, I am sure I enlisted because I wanted to become part of something big and important. Fighting for my country seemed like it would give my life meaning and purpose. As someone who was attracted to risk, I was ready to play the odds with gusto and courage. Of course, some use it as a stepping stone to a career or as a step to a higher status, to win the approval and admiration of those around or above them. It's possible that I was driven by many of those factors, but for me the primary reason was pride in my country.

In September I arrived at boot camp, where I learned discipline and how to follow orders. After six weeks of basic training and additional weeks of advanced training, I was stationed on the USS Northampton CC–1 (Communications Carrier), a light cruiser based in Norfolk, Virginia. The Northampton was one of two presidential flagships, meaning it was always available and on call for presidential use. For the first month, I served on the "mess deck," cleaning the ship's chow hall or dining area. A month later I was assigned to the radio room with the title of Radio Man Striker. Our communications team consisted of some twenty-one radio men, serving three eight-hour shifts. At any given time, there would be seven men on duty in the radio room.

On January 2, 1966, I was sent to Quantico, Virginia, under orders to go to Vietnam, where the life expectancy for a radio man was three minutes. Stationed south of Saigon, I was assigned to a riverboat, but after only three days on the field of battle, my communications vessel was hit by mortar from a shoreline battery. A piece of shrapnel from the boat hit my right knee, and for a month I was drugged up under a heavy dose of morphine. When I regained awareness, I was a patient at Portsmouth Naval Hospital in Virginia, the Navy's first and oldest continual naval hospital. I was placed in the psychiatric ward and diagnosed with PTSD. I was given the option to finish my military service early and be discharged, but I chose to stay for my entire four-year enlistment.

After release from the naval hospital, I was reassigned to the USS Wright CC–2, the sister ship to the Northampton. While serving as a radio man, we sailed to Punta del Este, Uruguay, a resort dubbed "The Miami Beach of South America," then hosting hemispheric summit meetings attended by U.S. President Lyndon Johnson. On the way, having crossed the equator, we took part in a special naval ceremony. Before first crossing the equator, sailors are called Polliwogs, but after crossing, they become Shellbacks.

In 1968, I was transferred to the Philadelphia Naval Yard, and the next year I became a "Plank Owner," joining ninety crew members in the commissioning of the guided-missile destroyer USS Mitscher DDG 35. In 1969 our ship's football team won the Philadelphia Naval Yard football championship and advanced to the finals for the East Coast naval championship game, which we lost 7–6.

While still in the Navy, it didn't take long for me to get married. I had met Jackie at my sister's wedding in 1967, and on February 10, 1968, while still enlisted and serving at the Philadelphia Naval Yard, we were married. After my discharge from the Navy in September 1969, I went to work for Bell Telephone Company, and in 1982 for its subsidiary AT&T (American Telephone and Telegraph). During that marriage, which lasted fifteen years, we had three miscarriages, but after ten years we were blessed with a daughter, whom we named Adrienne Decada. Her middle name was a testament to a decade of trying to conceive. Two years later, our son James David was born.

At this time I was involved in the masonic movement. In 1976, my friend Larry, a Pittsburgh policeman, had invited me to join the Freemasons, the oldest fraternal organization in the world. Having grown up in a blue-collar family, I was honored to participate in an organization that traced its origins to medieval workmen's guilds. Lacking stability in my personal life at that time, I maintained inconsistent membership with the Masons until 1995, when I began working my way through the ranks. In 1999 I rose to the top of the order in the Blue Lodge Chapter while rising up the ranks in other orders of York Right masonry, receiving membership in the Knights of the York Cross of Honour (KYCH). As an active participant in their programming and through their community outreach, I eventually became a Shriner in the Islamic Grotto, serving as Monarch while also doing charity work as a clown. This activity allowed me to bring joy to children and their parents. Though I still maintain membership in the Masons, my focus has now shifted.

Regretfully, I drank heavily during my marriage to Jackie, and in 1982 Jackie filed for divorce on the ground of neglect. When Jackie left me, she took the kids and married Charlie, my drinking companion and best friend. My mind was confused and I questioned my friend's loyalty, wondering how long he and my wife had been cheating on me. As it turned out, alcohol was my priority then, and I return to my alcoholic ways with a vengeance, thinking I could drink my way out of my troubles. In 2023, at my ex-wife's funeral and after having prayed for Jackie and our children, I came to realize that my best friend didn't abandon me. He had taken charge and married my ex-wife and raised my children. I am grateful to him and have told him so.

Sometimes it's good to hit rock bottom, because when you do, there's no lower point to go. Deciding to get help, I entered a recovery program, not to quit drinking, but to get my wife and kids back and to keep my job. I played a game with sobriety, entering and leaving my recovery program, not drinking, then drinking, not drinking, then drinking, and that went on from 1982 to 1984. One Saint Patrick's Day, I was invited to an Irish wedding. I woke up that day, took a shower, sorted through the dirty laundry to find something close to suitable to wear, and went to Joe's Tavern for breakfast. Having no intention of drinking that morning, I ordered ham and eggs, with potatoes and coffee.

When my meal came, I was shaking so badly I wasn't able to keep the food on my fork. The bartender saw my situation and came over to help. He said, "I know what you need," and he put a shot of alcohol in my coffee. I drank it and only then was able to eat my breakfast. I ordered another coffee and told the bartender I wanted more of what he had given me earlier. I felt I was off and running again.

At this point, I sat at the bar waiting for someone I knew to give me a ride to the wedding. As I sat finishing my drink, I noticed a man from my recovery group sitting at the bar eating. He had what seemed to me a drink in front of him and I thought, "What a hypocrite!" It was still easy to be critical of others, so long as I was not included.

When no one came in to give me a ride, I walked three miles to the wedding, stopping at several bars along the way. At the wedding, the host gave me a beer, and I went into a blackout. Later, when I asked the host if I had caused any problems, he told me that I had enjoyed myself and even had sex with a stranger. I was shocked, though I shouldn't have been, for during an alcoholic blackout one not only loses self-control, but has no recollection of what happened. The following morning someone knocked on my door, and it was my longtime friend Barbara. She was upset and began scolding me for drinking again. I kicked her out, but she came in through the back door. I kicked her out again, but she came in through the window. She just wanted to help, and all I wanted was to drink the sixpack in the fridge. Her persistence finally convinced me to get help.

I was desperate, and yet I didn't know what to do. She recommended I call my uncle Mike, who had been in recovery for thirty-nine years. When I called him, he said he would be glad to help. He told me to sit by the phone and not take another drink until he got back to me. An hour later I received a call from Gateway Rehab telling me they had a bed for me as long as I arrived before 9 p.m. I agreed. When I asked Barb if she would drive me there, she refused, saying she had to fix dinner for her husband.

When I got out of Gateway, I was still confused and immature The first two days I was in detox, followed by twenty-eight days of rehab, and it worked, for I have been sober now for thirty-nine years. Unfortunately, I still made some bad decisions. Soon after entering recovery, I married my childhood sweetheart Barbara. I had known her since the beginning of high school, and we had dated regularly until I enlisted in the Navy, at which time she had sent me a "Dear John" letter. Now, after divorcing her husband, she had custody of her three children, and they lived with us. We bought a diner, and I began working two jobs, AT&T from midnight until 8 a.m. and then at the diner until around 2 p.m, when I went home to sleep. I would get up for dinner, spend a few minutes with the family, and then back to bed. Obviously, such a lifestyle is a formula for failure, and despite our longtime friendship, the marriage did not last. After our divorce I went to live with my brother Moose.

In 1994, I experienced a genuine conversion to Jesus through the television ministry of Kenneth Copland. I had been a believer during my childhood, but that changed when I was twelve. During my marriage to Jackie, I continued attending church. As a Catholic, Jackie had our children baptized and confirmed as Catholics, but as a Protestant, I had the kids baptized Methodist. Despite my alcoholic ways, I became a trustee of my church and later, when a new minister came to our church, I was inspired to take my faith seriously by becoming a lay minister. However, despite undergoing the requisite training, I did not put my ministry into practice. My personal and married life were in disarray, and I was not yet ready for committed Christian service.

In 1986, two years after I stopped drinking, my sponsor in recovery told me, "Jim, there is a God, and you're not it!" That resonated with me, and I started to believe in a higher power. That became the start of my conversion. Having lost Jesus for twenty-five years, I reaffirmed my relationship with him, reclaiming the long-ignored image of God deep within me. Some people have an external, public conversion experience, but mine was primarily a private process. A significant part of this process, which I consider my first truly spiritual experience, was in 2007. I had recently had a left knee replaced, and I was alone in the car on my way to therapy. I was listening to a Christian talk show when suddenly the radio stopped. I remember praying then for my son and nephew, both addicted to drugs. As soon as I said, "Amen," the radio came back on, at which time I heard the talk show host say, "Don't worry about anything; pray about everything." The radio then shut down again and stopped working.

This experience fully convinced me in a higher power greater than myself, and that it was working in my life. From that point on, spirituality moved to the front burner of my life, and I became more God-focused and God-centered. Some people might question the existence of God, or the possibility of divine-human encounter, but for me this was clearly a "God moment."

Getting things straightened out with God prepared me for lasting commitment to Georgia Lee Brown, the love of my life. The happiest day of my life was when she accepted my proposal for marriage. We were married in November, 2000 and have been happily married since. Today age doesn't matter to me. When I was younger, I wanted to be older, and in my sixties, I wanted to be younger. Now I am content at the well-seasoned age of seventy-six.

Jim's Personality and Spirituality Profile

Jim's MBTI results are ESFJ. Unlike Georgia's dominant function, which is "F," Jim's dominant is "S." Nevertheless, Jim and Georgia's other functions are identical, meaning they have much in common. Described as Consul, Jim is a person with Extraverted, Sensing, Feeling, and Judging personality traits. Consuls are attentive and people-focused, participating fully in their social community. Their achievements are guided by decisive values, and they willingly offer guidance to others.

For Consuls, life is sweetest when it is shared with others. Hence, Jim has always sought the company of others, be they male or female friends, and felt most fulfilled in marriage, or, in his case, in consecutive marriages. People with this personality type form the bedrock of many communities, opening their homes—and their hearts—to friends, loved ones, and neighbors. This doesn't mean that Consuls like everyone, or that they're saints. However, Consuls do believe in the power of hospitality and good manners, and they tend to feel a sense of duty to those around them. Generous and reliable, people with this personality type often take it upon themselves to hold their families and their communities together.

Like Protagonists, Consuls are altruistic. They take seriously their responsibilities to give back, serve others, and do the right thing. And Consuls believe there is a clear right thing to do in nearly every situation. While some personality types adopt a more lenient, live-and-let-live attitude, Consuls may find it difficult not to judge when someone takes a path that strikes them as misguided. As a result, Consuls often struggle to accept it when someone—particularly someone they care about—disagrees with them. With their definite views on right and wrong, Consuls tend to be on the opinionated side. However, these opinions aren't arbitrary—they are often based on a deep respect for tradition. Consuls know that everything they do affects someone else, and they trust that established laws, protocols, and social norms will help them navigate their everyday lives in a way that is considerate and responsible toward others.

Supportive and outgoing, Consults are frequently highly visible at a party, always around making sure that everyone else is having a good time. However, they should not be judged as flighty; just the opposite, they are loyal to the core, building meaningful relationships, and they can be counted on to show up whenever a helping hand—or a listening ear—is needed. Hence, in therapy or recovery groups, they are regularly valued for their friendship and care.

With their love of order and structure, Consuls prefer planned events to open-ended activities or spontaneous get-togethers—and they are happy to host in order to ensure that everything goes smoothly. People with this personality type put a great deal of energy into making other people feel special and celebrated, and they may take it personally when someone doesn't seem to appreciate their efforts.

ESFJs have strong practical skills, and they are excellent managers of everyday tasks and routines. Valuing stability and security, they have a strong sense of responsibility and strive to meet their obligations. Eager to preserve the status quo, they are true pillars of any groups they belong to. Helping to ensure stability, Consul personalities seek harmony and care deeply about other people's feelings, being careful not to offend or hurt others. Good at connecting with others, they are strong team players. Being social, easygoing, and well-liked, Consul personalities have a strong need to "belong," and have no problem following social cues in order to help them take an active role in their communities.

Despite their many strengths, Consuls are often preoccupied with social status and influence, which affects many decisions they make, potentially limiting their creativity and open-mindedness. Critical of people outside the mainstream, Consuls may also be unwilling to step out of their own comfort zones, usually for fear of being (or appearing) different. Being conflict-averse, Consul personalities can become defensive or hurt if someone, especially a person close to them, criticizes their habits, beliefs, or traditions. On account of their sensitivity to the needs and views of others, Consuls often neglect their own needs in the process.

Prizing social validation and belonging so highly, romantic relationships hold a special level of importance for Consuls. No other kind of relationship provides people with the Consul personality type with the same level of support and devotion, and the feelings of security and stability that come with strong romantic relationships are extremely validating. With such a goal in mind, ESFJ personalities take each stage in romantic relationship very seriously. Everything about their relationships is based on satisfying mutual needs, from creating understanding early on to building mutual respect and support for each other's opinions and goals. Knowing that they are loved and appreciated has a huge effect on their mood and self-esteem.

If they feel like this support isn't there, such as when their partners deliver criticism, ESFJs can feel extremely hurt. People with the Consul personality type dislike conflict and criticism, which can make it challenging to address any problems that come up. Nothing is more hurtful or depressing to Consuls than to realize that their partners don't respect their dreams or opinions. Consuls can be surprisingly tough and tireless in the face of hardship, but they need to know that their partners have their backs. Unfortunately, less mature Consuls may lack the inner strength and wisdom to attract this in healthy ways. They can be very needy, compromising their own principles and values in exchange for their partners' approval. This is a terrible trap—not only is it unattractive, it can too easily lead to emotionally abusive relationships, which reduce Consuls' self-esteem further. Another snare is their fixation on social status and approval—it is not uncommon for Consuls' social circles and relatives to play a bigger part in their choice of dating partners than even their own values. As sensors, Consuls are centered on the physical world and tend to be quite emotional and affectionate. People with this personality type love to find ways to make their partners happy.

Consuls are a very social personality type, seeking large circles of friends and proving themselves more than willing to spend the time and energy necessary to maintain these relationships. Loyal and warm, Consuls are known for standing by their friends no matter what, and providing a constant source of emotional support and encouragement. Doing everything they can to make sure others are happy, Consults are naturally popular in most any environment, and hence, may frequently be placed in positions of leadership.

Because they are well-organized and enjoy bringing order and structure to their workplaces, careers as administrators are a natural fit. However, purely analytical careers are often too dull for Consuls, for they need human interaction and emotional feedback to be truly satisfied in their work. Good listeners and enthusiastic team members, ESFJs are excellent providers for people in need. Comfortable with authority, they can also be supportive and friendly enough to keep that authority from feeling overbearing. Few personality types are as practical and caring as Consuls. Known for their social and administrative skills, Consuls are good at creating and maintaining a secure, stable, and friendly environment for themselves and their loved ones.

Typed on the Enneagram as a Type Three (dominant) with a Two "wing" (auxiliary), Jim's Enneagram type is practically identical to Georgia's, only her reverse. As we noted in Georgia's profile, Type Threes, known as Achievers or Performers, are self-assured, attractive, and charming. Their primary virtue is *Truthfulness*. Ambitious, competent, and energetic, they can also be status-conscious and highly driven for personal advancement. Threes are often concerned about their image and what others think of them. They typically have problems with workaholism and competitiveness. Their primary passion is *Vanity* or deceit, putting effort into developing their ego instead of their true nature. At their best, healthy Threes are self-accepting, authentic, and everything they seem to be—role models who inspire others. Type Twos, also known as Helpers or Givers, are empathetic, sincere, and warm-hearted. Their primary virtue is *Humility*. They are friendly, generous, and self-sacrificing, but they can also be sentimental, flattering, and people-pleasing. They are driven to be close to others, and they often do things for others in order to be needed. They typically have problems taking care of themselves and acknowledging their own needs. Their primary Passion is *Pride*, better described as Vainglory—pride in their own virtue. At their best, healthy Twos are unselfish and altruistic and have unconditional love for themselves and others.

As an ESFJ, Jim's spirituality type is "SF." As noted in chapter 2,

> SFs are characterized by an *experience-based spirituality*. SF youth make friends easily, avoid conflict, and desire to please. They thrive in well-structured environments and when expectations are clear. They need to be reassured when they are on the right track and rewarded for good behavior. As adults SFs are sensitive, loyal, and caring; they live responsibly as

> parents and citizens and are devoted to serving others in tangible ways. Instead of the cosmic, the tangible task at hand is the focus. Details are important. Stressing continuity and propriety, SFs are traditionalists. In their communications they prefer anecdotes, stories, and tangible references to symbolic or abstract reasoning. Practical and interactive, they take a tactile, hands-on approach to the spiritual life.

Combining Urban Holmes' Spirituality Wheel and John Westerhoff's approach, as an "S," Jim's spiritual typological preference is Type I: speculative-kataphatic or sacramental. This type, an intellectual, "thinking" spirituality, aids persons in fulfilling their vocation in the world. This spirituality favors what it can see, touch, and vividly imagine.

6

Life Together

Georgia and Jim's Story

Georgia's Perspective

In my early thirties, my best friend Marybeth kept telling me about an awesome guy named Jim. Both of us were single at the time, and she seemed to be smitten by him. In the spring of 1996, when I was thirty-five and three years sober, Marybeth and I attended a semiannual conference for recovering alcoholics at Cook Forest State Park, a beautiful 8,500-acre site with cabins and a lodge in northwestern Pennsylvania.

When Marybeth introduced me to Jim and I looked into his crystal-blue eyes, I was instantly hooked. Jim exuded an energy and warmth that I found both irresistible and alarming, for being laid-back, I felt overwhelmed by his intense energy. Though I had never met someone so energetic, I also sensed he was a sincere, caring individual and a person who truly loved God, and that was a wonderful but scary combination. Whenever I am attracted to someone, I feel afraid, and that's when I knew Jim was special, because I felt afraid. However, over time his love of surprise and his sense of humor became endearing qualities, and it was clear that he loved others because he felt loved by God.

Jim was employed at the time, and he was living with his brother and a Vietnam veteran in Vandergrift, Pennsylvania, about one and one-half hours from my home. Despite being separated from his wife, Jim was still legally married at the time, though both agreed that they would see other people. Despite the difference in years between us—I was thirty-four and

Jim was forty-eight—age did not seem a factor, for Jim had twice the energy of anyone I knew. At one point, after I had left home and was moving into an apartment, Jim and his brother came to help me move, and they brought a waterbed for me to use. Jim and I both had two jobs, so we didn't have much free time to date. Our first official date was when we traveled together to attend a conference for recovering alcoholics in Toronto, Canada.

In 1996, after Jim and I began dating regularly, the house next door to my mother's house came up for sale, and thinking Jim could stay with me and be closer to work than where he was living with his brother, I decided it made sense to stop paying rent and invest in a home. Living next to my mother would also make it much easier to care for her. The timing was remarkable, for my grandmother died later that year, and I was able to be near her in her final days. In 1999, a few years after Jim had moved in with me, my sister returned from California with her husband and three children and needed a place to stay. We had plenty of room and with Jim's approval, we invited them to live with us. Meanwhile, my mother lived next door, often with questionable companionship, for she frequently invited drug addicted acquaintances to stay with her. As a mentally unstable alcoholic, she often made poor decisions, but she never stopped caring for people in need.

When Terry Eger, my friend and boss at the nursing home, heard that Jim was living with me, she told me that being unmarried and living with a single man did not set a good example for Sissy's children. Though Jim and I were now committed Christians, we were still "baby Christians," and we didn't see anything wrong with living together. Despite understanding Terry's point, I had been avoiding a wedding because I was insecure and afraid. I wanted a wedding, but I feared being the center of attention. Nevertheless, the time had come to conquer my fears and to live responsibly as a more mature Christian. Having decided on a wedding, I wanted it to be private, but as my confidence grew, I became more willing to challenge myself by leaving my comfort zone, and now I am very glad I had a bigger public wedding. Jim and I set the wedding for November 4, 2000 at our small home church, Gladden United Presbyterian Church. Having a public wedding allowed the residents of the nursing home where I worked to get involved, both with the wedding plans and in the ceremony itself, and my family and friends all helped to make this a memorable event.

After my marriage to Jim, Sissy, now divorced, moved back next door to live with our mother. In 2001, when her house caught fire and suffered significant damage, Sissy and her three children moved back in with us.

When the home was rebuilt, Sissy and her kids moved back, but this time Mom stayed with Jim and me until her death in 2015.

As a recently married thirty-nine-year-old, I wished to be a mother. I had always wanted children, and that desire had been heightened in 1990, when I had left home to live with my friend Jenny in her apartment on Grandview Avenue in Mount Washington, with a scenic view of downtown Pittsburgh. Her father, a prominent judge, had helped her acquire an apartment in this exclusive location, but she needed a roommate. Her influential contacts offered to help me get a better paying job, but I was content with my current circumstances, for I wished to remain independent and in control of my life. As a teenager, I had learned that material wealth and success didn't necessarily translate into personal happiness. Controlling my schedule was also important, for I wanted to be available in case my mother or grandmother needed my help.

At this time, my niece Julia was born to my brother Jim. At her birth, his wife Sandy, like my mother at the birth of Jim, suffered from postpartum depression, and as often happens with persons diagnosed with psychotic depression, this condition often leads to erratic thought and dangerous and negligent behavior. My brother Jim was serving on a naval base in San Diego, California at this time, and when his wife was institutionalized, he took Matt, then two years old, to live with his aunt Helen, and he brought baby Julia to live with Jenny and me in Grandview Avenue. Although this arrangement was temporary, it proved difficult for me, since I was working two jobs and had no financial support for the baby. However, during this time, Jenny and I learned what it was like to care for an infant.

Three months later, when Sandy was released from her hospitalization, I returned Julia to her care. However, despite this brief experience, surrogate motherhood suited me, for upon giving her back to her mother, I too went into depression. Feeling guilty for placing Julia into a fragile situation, and suffering from alcoholism, I submitted to medical evaluation and was briefly institutionalized. Released after a week of care, I was encouraged to undergo alcohol treatment at Gateway rehabilitation center. My mother, also an alcoholic, encouraged me to go, and knowing that I loved to swim, enticed me with promises that Gateway had a pool. However, as everyone knew, there was no pool at Gateway. Feeling responsible for workers dependent upon me in my cleaning business, I declined admittance to Gateway, and I was able to continue working, which was a good thing, for keeping busy helped take my mind away from Julia and her broken family.

Feeling lonely and depressed, I needed someone or something to care for, so I purchased an old horse and kept him at a farm nearby.

Julia was now living with her single mom, recently divorced from Jim. After a short time, the children were placed in Jim's care. Needing help, Jim returned to western Pennsylvania, traveling cross-country with them in a beat-up old Volkswagen van. When he arrived, I was at the farm with my horse and Matt ran toward me from the car. This gave me such a good feeling, and I bonded with him instantly, as I had earlier with Julia. I had moved back home with my grandmother and mother, and this time we all took care of them. For two and a half years, four generations were under one roof.

In 2001, when I became pregnant, I was ready to become a mother. I had heard that it was safe and somewhat common for women to have children in their forties, but what I didn't know was that many of those cases involved in vitro fertilization and gestational or host surrogacy. Jim had already fathered two children with his first wife, so he was not overly interested in fathering additional children, but knowing that this was important to me, he heeded a friend's advice, "If you want to get along, go along." After a month of pregnancy, a test confirmed the results, and Jim and I began sharing the good news with others.

However, after eight or nine weeks, I had a miscarriage, and since I was still smoking heavily, I blamed myself for the miscarriage. I had begun smoking in high school, and gradually became addicted until it peaked in 2008, when I was smoking two and a half packs a day, a habit that cost me $800 a month. Smoking had been a way of life in my family for generations, and growing up with my grandfather and grandmother Brinley, both smokers together with my mom, and being genetically predisposed to smoking, I easily replicated their behavior. Although I am now smoke free, quitting was a difficult process. The seed for quitting had been planted by friends over time, but the decisive moment for me came when I had lung surgery. My mother had died from a combination of factors, including lung cancer. She and I shared the same doctor, so when I went for a checkup and had a cough, my doctor recommended that I get a chest X-ray.

Due to a growth on my lung and blood in my urine, my thoracic doctor recommended a PET-CT scan. Though the results came back negative, he questioned the results, and advised surgery. I agreed, deciding that this would be my opportunity to quit smoking. In 2018 I quit smoking, and have remained smoke-free ever since.

Before our marriage, Jim had been commissioned as a lay minister in the Methodist Church, but after 2000, he transferred his church membership to Gladden United Presbyterian Church, where we had been married. He quickly became involved in the work of our local church, serving as trustee and later as an elder on session. Earlier, I had taught Sunday School at Gladden, and after my marriage, I too served on session.

The year 2008 was a tragic one for our extended family, for that was the year my nephew Matt was "killed by action" (KBA) in Afghanistan. At that time the United States was going through a heroin crisis and many young people were dying; soldiers were completing suicide at the rate of twenty-two per day. Emotionally involved with Matt at this time, I felt a deep desire to help, and I can honestly say that without Jesus, scripture, and my husband, I would not have survived my grief.

After having returned from California as a single dad, my brother Jim, together with Matt and Julia, had moved in with my grandmother, mother, and me. Around 1992, Jim took the kids to live with our father Ron Brown while Jim enrolled in Allegheny Community College and later at the University of Pittsburgh, where he earned a degree as an electrical engineer. As Ron tells the story, Jim dressed the children every morning before carting them off to a day care center, and he was there for them whenever they were sick or awakened from nightmares.

In 2006, when Matt graduated from high school, he joined the military. For many generations, our family had been a military family, and more recently that tradition included both grandfathers, my uncles, my father, my husband, my brother-in-law, my brother Jim, my sister, and myself. Sissy and I had both enlisted after college, and while Sissy served in the army reserves from 1984–1989, I did so temporarily, in part so I could pay off student loans. Upon taking the entrance exams, I learned that I had achieved sufficiently high scores to pay off my loans. I signed up for delayed entry and began to work in design, though I had achieved a high score in linguistics. Since I had no idea what that meant, I chose design instead. Being several pounds overweight, I never made it to basic training. Since it was peace time, I was allowed to take part in certain activities while I worked on my weight. I had three months to comply, but I used this time unwisely, eating and drinking compulsively. Unable to lose weight, I was allowed to exit gracefully. The army had its standards, and I didn't qualify. In addition to my compulsive eating and drinking, I was also scared, so I didn't give it my best effort.

Perhaps my attitude helps explain Matt's experience in the military. Like other members of his family, he had enlisted in the army, often a choice for people with low self-esteem. He had been recruited directly from high school, having enlisted without consulting his family. And he was placed in the 82nd Airborne Division, a tough division of the army. Despite being well trained, he was a shy, gentle individual, poorly suited for combat.

In hindsight, he might better have served in a more peaceful endeavor, such as AmeriCorps or Peace Corps, although initially he seemed to be up for the challenge. When he enlisted, he was not particularly fearful of death or even of fighting, but when he got a taste of combat in boot camp, fear took over. As a high school graduate, he certainly had options, but having done poorly in school, joining the military became a path of least resistance—they give you a test, and if you pass, you're in. At that point, recruits feel their life has purpose, and they believe this experience will prepare them for a better future. In addition, Matt was building on a family legacy, because that's what young men in his family had done.

Twice during training, first in boot camp and later during advanced training, Matt went AWOL, and on those occasions, he came back to live with Jim and me. The first occasion lasted a couple of months, but with legal assistance, he was able to return to the military. The second time he was sentenced to time in jail, but he was released soon thereafter because the army needed boots on the ground in Afghanistan. Matt was in a bad state at that time, for in addition to being mentally troubled and confused, he had addiction issues.

When Matt returned to the military, he stayed on drugs. In Afghanistan, he was part of Operation Freedom, classified as a medical and humanitarian mission. During his brief service abroad, Matt lived with a great deal of guilt. As is frequently the case, it is natural to place blame or guilt on others. For me in college, when I got depressed, it was the college's fault; for people in the military, it's the military's fault. I saw the struggle in Matt, and my husband Jim saw it as well. It is easy for parents, relatives, and close friends to live in denial when a loved one is on drugs, but given our background with drugs and our commitment to sobriety, Jim and I knew. There is no question that Matt was living with fear; his life was chaotic, and his future, both in Afghanistan and after service, was uncertain and insecure.

In Afghanistan, Matt became separated from his unit when he volunteered to serve as a prison guard. He was stationed near Kabul, among the most dangerous places in the world at the time. While on duty, he saw incarcerated twelve-year-old Afghan boys that had been recruited by al-Qaeda and the Taliban to fight against the Americans. These boys cried constantly, were uneducated, malnourished and uncared for, and were highly traumatized. In addition, Matt regularly saw men who had carried dead bodies for miles, thinking they could be revived.

Afghanistan was a whole different world for a sensitive, impressionable, unstable eighteen-year-old like Matt. And taking alcohol and drugs to cope only made conditions worse. On one occasion, he returned to Pennsylvania on leave, and when we saw him, he was a different person. One day, back on guard duty in Afghanistan, he completed suicide. His funeral was a difficult time for the entire family. His death made the news, and reporters began calling us regularly for updates. A large crowd showed up for his funeral, which included a military burial.

During his eulogy, his grandfather Ron Brown mentioned how he had given Matt an old Bible for comfort and protection. It was a special Bible, a pocket edition carried by a Civil War captain named John L. Nelson through all four years of the conflict. Research reveals that this Bible accompanied its owner through such storied battles as Nashville, Shiloh, Vicksburg, Chickamauga, and Atlanta. It had even traveled with Captain Nelson's 30th Illinois Infantry Division on General Sherman's march to the sea. And reasoning that the Bible had protected Captain Nelson throughout the carnage of that great war, Ron assumed it would protect Matt as well.

A passage had been marked in Captain Nelson's Bible, the only passage thus marked in that King James Version. From that passage, Ron highlighted two phrases from verses 7 and 8: "The Lord shall keep thy soul," and "forever will," and in his eulogy, he indicated that while this passage does not promise divine protection from earthly calamities, it does promise eternal protection of one's "soul." When I brought this interpretation to Dr. Vande Kappelle, he told me that ancient Hebrew people, as modern Jews, have a unified anthropology, meaning they do not compartmentalize human beings into body, soul, or spirit, so that when the word "soul" appears in the Hebrew scriptures, it is merely a synonym for "person" or "life." This interpretation is also corroborated by textual evidence, for the psalms often use what is called poetic or synonymous parallelism, as can be seen in Psalm 121:7, where the first and second part of the verse repeat the same idea, only using different words. Hence, as the NRSV reads, "The Lord will keep you from all evil; he will keep your life" (121:7), translating "soul" by "you" and "thee" by "your life."[1]

In the fall of 2016, the year after my mother's death, Jim joined me at my college homecoming reunion. Feeling free from my lifelong commitment to care for needy relatives, I was ready to embark on a new adventure. It was at a homecoming luncheon that I reconnected with Dr. Van, my college religion professor. He had recently published *Securing Life*, an overview of biblical themes, and I was ready for a new spiritual challenge. Dr. Van encouraged me to start a study group, so Jim and I began inviting friends in recovery and others at church and nearby to join us. Soon a group of around fifteen people began meeting weekly to study Dr. Van's books. Inspired, intrigued, and challenged by *Securing Life*, our next book was *Grace Revealed*, Dr. Van's commentary on Paul's letter to the Romans.

A few years later, when I attended Billy Burke's healing services and experienced comprehensive healing, I recall hearing Pastor Burke's teaching that God prepares people for healing beforehand, "It's what you do before you get here that matters," and I credit studying *Grace Revealed* for my healing, for on the occasion of my physical healing, I felt God's grace, and it was an awesome experience. Reading *Grace Revealed* was God's preparation for my healing, and today I continue to receive guidance from both Body in Spirit—the name we have given to our study group—and World Outreach—Billy Burke's organization.

Body in Spirit has changed my life by bringing me into second half of life spirituality. Through this study I have become a better witness, sharing my faith and communicating my views and beliefs with greater subtlety and hence more winsomeness. I've become more tolerant and respectful of other people's views, and have received more insight into my own perspectives and views. I've also learned that it is okay to question, because God does answer, and questioning is how we grow. Through Body in Spirit I have grown closer to Jesus, and discovered how to live with purpose. I have also learned a great deal about my personality type and that of others, and

1. At this point I wish to make clear that when Georgia heard my explanation, she responded as a well-educated person of faith might respond, "Isn't it possible that ancient Hebrews had a limited view of theology and anthropology, and that the views of the King James translators might reveal a progressive or heightened view of the topic not yet understood by ancient Jews?" Knowing that this is a view used by Jewish scholars over the years, namely, that all revelation was given in biblical times, including many ideas that scholarly believers might uncover only in later times, I can only marvel at Georgia's faithful response. Am I right? Is Georgia right? Who can speak of such things definitively, things only God knows?

this has allowed me to become a facilitator of growth for other participants in our group.

In addition, studying scripture and spirituality in an open, nonthreatening way has brought me mental and spiritual healing. In the course of my study I have discovered two transformative teachings from these books: (1) that heaven is not only a future hope but also a present reality, and (2) that human beings are cocreators with God. While keeping me grounded and balanced, Dr. Van's books have enlarged my horizons. Likewise, they have given me a greater understanding of personal freedom, and how our freedom must be tempered by respect and responsibility. I have also learned that healthy spirituality is not a solo endeavor, but relational, for it bonds us with God and with others. Reading scripture, I've discovered, also bonds us to others because it provides a common foundation upon which we can build community. As Christians understand it, this is the work of the Holy Spirit, who binds us through scripture, study, prayer, sharing, and corporate worship.

The healing I have experienced is the result of the growth and maturity that comes through second half of life living, thinking, and being. Second half of life relationships reduce stress because, like marriage, sharing faith and life heightens our joys and diminishes our sorrows. I consider the high point in my relationship with Jim to be right now, just the two of us alone at last (together with our four cats and a dog), living together, working together, and studying together. How many people get to share all this with their spouse? Often spouses do these things apart or with others, and we are blessed to be able to share so much and in such depth.

When we cocreate with one another, as Jim and I do in Body in Spirit, we cocreate with God. Convening and directing our study group has led this group to form an art group whose mission is to encourage participants to be cocreators with God. When we create art, we celebrate not only our individual gifts but also celebrate the gifts God gives us as a body, and we use these gifts to inspire and bless our friends, neighbors, and our surrounding community. In my case, art has become a catalyst to set up art workshops in nearby nursing homes. The joint exercises I devise for the residents are enjoyable while giving them an opportunity to express themselves. Our work leads to art shows, which provide a sense of accomplishment for residents who might otherwise feel inferior, despondent, or insecure.

When I consider my personal qualities, my best quality is my gift to love and care for others. When I see other people, I see them as created by

God and in God's image. I say that love is a gift because when I allow Jesus to love others through me, everything works out better. As I learned recently from research on dogs conducted by Vanessa Woods and Brian Hare at Duke University and reported in their book, *Survival of the Friendliest*, dog species that have thrived and survived evolved from ancient wolves due to their capacity for friendliness. Likewise, for the approximately 300,000 years that *Homo sapiens* have existed, human beings have shared the planet with at least four other types of humans. All of these were smart, strong, and inventive. However, around 50,000 years ago, *Homo sapiens* made a cognitive leap that gave us an edge over other species. What happened? Since Charles Darwin wrote about "evolutionary fitness," the idea of fitness has been confused with physical strength, tactical brilliance, and aggression. In fact, what made human beings evolutionarily fit was a remarkable kind of friendliness, a virtuosic ability to coordinate and communicate with others that allowed us to achieve many cultural and technical accomplishments throughout human history. Despite my many faults, some passed on from distant and also more directly from ancestors such as my mother, I believe it is the quality of empathy, expressed through compassion and kindness and modeled for us in the life of Jesus, that defines and shapes me at my best.

As all who know him can attest, Jim's best quality is his sense of humor and his natural ability to care for others. He is loyal, tenacious, and reliable, and I am blessed to be his mate. While Jim and I are compatible in many ways, we are also significantly different in other ways. Whereas I need to talk things out, Jim is more easily satisfied with things as they are, and he doesn't need to introspect as much as I do. Jim is not a talker, but I believe that is true of men in general. According to one source, women speak 24,000 words a day, whereas most men only 6,000. When Jim talks with friends on the phone, his conversations last around two minutes. When I talk, it is often for an hour or more, and that seems natural to us women.

When I look to the future, I am hopeful for our Body in Spirit group. Even if we don't grow numerically, we will continue growing spiritually, emotionally, intellectually, and even socially. After having spent several years in study, our group is now looking for ways to make our neighborhood stronger and better, and we have started by cleaning up litter in South Fayette Township. We are becoming more socially and racially diverse, and have begun studying topics such as racism. In addition, we have sponsored talks, ecumenical church visits, and programs associated with Black history. Individually, I am becoming more involved with Billy Burke's World Outreach organization, including attending meetings and participating in prayer for individuals and for our world in general. These projects have increased hope for myself and the future, hope that I am not too old to make a difference in my world. Recently, I have explored finishing my college education, and I am making a difference in nursing homes and through my talent for art and painting.

Prayer—spoken and unspoken—is giving me strength and wisdom for the journey ahead, and I am learning the secret of praying without ceasing (see 1 Thessalonians 5:17). I have come to consider prayer like breathing—I pray all day long. I find that the combination of contemplation and action keeps me running on all cylinders—physically, emotionally, and spiritually. Knowing Jesus, staying connected with him, and allowing him to love others through me keeps me going and growing. Jesus is my best friend, but as I said earlier, this is not a solo relationship, because friendship with Jesus gives me a healthier perspective of life, greater self-respect, and endless love for all God's creatures—two-legged and four-legged alike—particularly those in need.

In terms of recreation, I enjoy gardening, going for walks, cycling, and swimming. I watch television selectively, and that goes for all news and social media, and I focus on filling my life with biblical values and teaching. I am more aware now of what I put into my mind, and I take responsibility for my thoughts and actions. That is a major change from my smoke and alcohol addicted days, and I feel like a new person—a healthier, younger, more positive and more energetic individual. As a citizen of God's kingdom, I am an instrument of God's love, an agent of well-being to myself and those around me. I listen and look for inspiration, and when I hear what I need to hear and see what I need to see, I don't need to do so repetitively. Living on that level of awareness saves me a great deal of time and energy and allows me to focus on spiritual priorities—loving God and others as extensions of myself.

In her writings on spirituality, the fifteenth-century Spanish mystic Teresa of Ávila wrote regularly about the transformative power of divine love. In love with every dimension of life, with people and places, music, laughter and celebration, and like the great Francis of Assisi, in love with nature and its abundance, Teresa taught her readers how to live the human adventure with zest and enthusiasm. In one of her writings, she shares a major second half of life discovery: "Remember, if you want to make progress on the path [of spirituality] and ascend to the places you have longed for, the important thing is not to think much but to love much, and so to do whatever best awakens you to [divine] love."[2]

Jim's Perspective

The spring of 1996 I attended a conference for recovering alcoholics at Cook Forest State Park, located several hours north of Pittsburgh. I was in my cabin relaxing with friends when an acquaintance named Marybeth stopped by. She introduced me to her friend Georgia Lee Brown, and when I met her, she took my breath away. She was beautiful, intelligent, highly energetic, and full of swagger, and I immediately fell in love.

After visiting her and seeing her at recovery meetings, Georgia joined me for a drive to Toronto to another recovery conference. I took her out to dinner but asked her if we could go Dutch, because I was broke. Happily, she laughed and agreed, and we continued dating for three years. One afternoon she and I were cutting the grass at my rental property. She was sweating and covered with grass and I was smitten, because it was then that I asked her to marry me.

The year 2000 began a new millennium, and for me, it was both the end of the old and the beginning of the new, for I retired from my job at AT&T in September, got divorced in October, and married Georgia on November 4. Two weeks later I began partnering with her in Capital Cleaning Service, and by faith and with divine help we have remained happily married for twenty-three years. During that period we have worked together, worshipped together, and collaborated in numerous community endeavors.

For the past ten years I have served as president of the board of Rebus House, a half-way house for recovering alcoholics. The house has a manager, a cook, and provides room for twenty-one residents. Although we have not been blessed with children of our own, Georgia and I support numerous charities, including World Outreach, Navigators, Boys Town, the Humane Society, St. Joseph's Indian School, and our local Gladden United Presbyterian Church.

In 2017, Georgia and I began a study group called Body in Spirit, sponsoring this group under guidance from our mentor and friend Robert Vande Kappelle (Dr. Van), whose books we read and study. I find these resources provide me with the education I either missed or neglected earlier

2. Teresa of Ávila, *Interior Castle*, 91.

in my life. In addition, at the start of the COVID epidemic in 2019, Georgia and I started a daily online recovery meeting, a support group that continues to this day, particularly for shut-ins who are not physically able to attend meetings.

Although I have suffered from ADD and ADHD since childhood and was diagnosed with PTSD during combat in Vietnam, I am grateful that God has blessed me these latter years with spiritual clarity and vision, and has given me the strength and endurance to commit to a mission of love and service to others, sharing God's blessings with people in need. I consider the high point in my relationship with Georgia to be seeing the spark in her eyes when we got married. The minister had said, "Look in each other's eyes, and picture your future," and I saw a spark in Georgia's eyes, a spark of hope and enthusiasm for what lay ahead.

When I examine my personal qualities, I consider my best quality to be my ability to work with others and to care for those in need. God has given me a gift of listening and caring, and I express that gift through charitable work and by living responsible. In our relationship, Georgia and I treat one another equally and respectfully. Georgia takes the initiative in some things, and I in others. We both cook and share in household chores, although this continues to be a work in progress at times. I consider Georgia's best quality to be organization, a quality I often find lacking in myself.

My hope for the future is to keep working with Georgia as a team, and to continue caring for one another. Being fourteen years older that Georgia, I don't want to become a burden on her. I hope to continue growing intellectually and spiritually, and I wish to do everything in my power to keep Body in Spirit going. I am grateful that God has preserved my life to the point where I could begin entering the second half of life spiritually, and I look forward to benefitting from all the resources of God's kingdom in my remaining years on earth and for all eternity.

Eventually I would like to help make possible the opening of a detox center for struggling addicts. When I look at the greater Pittsburgh area, I find only two detox centers functioning with adequate professional trained staff. However, unlike most detox centers, I would like to introduce spirituality as an option and not have the setting be exclusively secular.

7

Helen's Story[1]

In 2012, shortly after my marriage to Bob, my doctor discovered a tumor growing on my thyroid. Then local doctors referred me to an endocrinologist in Pittsburgh for surgery. On my way to Pittsburgh, I was emotionally overwhelmed. Overworked and tired, I prayed for a sign of God's existence. It was winter, and I was alone in my car. Tears poured from my face as I cried to God, "Are you there, God?" I needed a sign; would I receive it? Snow had recently fallen and I stopped at a convenience store outside of Altoona for coffee. The snowfall had been particularly high here, and I stopped my car thinking, "I'll buy a lottery ticket while I wait for my coffee." I had never played the lottery, but I thought, if I win the lottery, this will be my sign from God.

It was still early in the morning, and the snow had not yet been shoveled. As I plodded through the snow, I saw an object glistening at my feet. Bending down to pick it up, I discovered it was a St. Christopher medallion made of 18-caret gold. A family stood nearby, and thinking one of them had dropped it I asked, "Is this yours?" When they said it wasn't theirs, I entered the store, asking if anyone had lost the medallion, but no one had.

While the Christopher medal is viewed by Catholics as providing safety to travelers, it has become popular for people of all religious backgrounds. According to legend, Saint Christopher devoted his life to carry

1. For those reading this book for the first time or who want background on Helen's story, it is helpful to read chapter 4 (Georgia's story) first for context. On the other hand, Helen's story also amplifies and completes elements of their combined story. As noted in chapter 4, the name Sissy in that chapter refers to Helen, whereas in this chapter, the name Sissy refers to Georgia.

the weak and poor across a river. One night, when he was carrying a child, he felt his burden grow heavier with each step. When questioned, the child declared that he was the Christ and that Christopher was thus bearing the weight of the world.

At that point I decided to keep the medallion, for it was then that I recognized it as the sign that God was with me. I didn't even bother buying a lottery ticket, for I felt I had won the lottery. The fact that I found the medallion was in itself amazing, for I am not a sensor like Bob. When he heard my story, he asked, "How did you find it? You don't notice anything!" Needless to say, I made it to Pittsburgh safely that day and my experience with thyroid surgery went well. But more importantly, I felt God was by my side then and always, and that I need never again be disappointed.

• • •

When my mother was pregnant with my brother Jimmy (Sissy and I were about two and a half years old at the time), my dad brought a visitor home. It was after dinner and my mother entered the living room with a tray of pastries, when suddenly she became upset and started yelling. Mom often had fits of anger, and on this occasion she screamed at my dad, dropped the tray—or possibly threw it—and stormed out of the room. Embarrassed, Dad put his head down, and didn't say anything. Knowing we needed security, Dad had been trying to get life insurance on my mom. As I learned later, our visitor was an insurance agent.

There was nothing predictable about my mother's life and behavior. She was sweet and gentle most of the time, but had occasional explosive outbursts I can only explain as rage. At times she would throw oranges at us and once she locked Sissy in the trunk of our car. She nearly died when she delivered us. She was told not to have more children, so her pregnancy and delivery of Jimmy went poorly. Eventually, she was diagnosed with psychotic postpartum depression, which resulted in severe mood swings and erratic behavior.

The event that got her institutionalized took place when Jimmy was only a couple of months old. A neighborhood dog regularly got into our garbage, and one time I ran to my mother and told her the dog was back. Enraged, she took a kitchen knife and went outside and stabbed the dog. As it turned out, the dog belonged to the family of a fifteen-year-old boy who was molesting Sissy and me. While the dog was raiding her garbage, the boy was abusing her daughters. Thus, while an observer might only have witnessed my mother's violent behavior, the full picture was that she had learned of the boy's sexual advances, which she addressed several times with no cessation. As she told me later, "I couldn't get this boy to stop molesting you!" My dad had talked to the boy on at least two occasions, and had even talked to his parents, and the molestation still didn't stop. However, no one had called the authorities, for back then, people tended to excuse such behavior as something boys did.

Desperate and depressed, my mom had stabbed that dog to protect us, and it worked, for after that, the boy stopped molesting us—though it was the dog that paid the price. In addition, my dad was having an affair at work—and for all that was going on emotionally in her life, my mother did the only thing she knew to do—stop the abuse. She was staying true to her Machiavellian motto, "You have to make people afraid of you." Obviously, limits must be placed on certain actions, for when someone is in an altered state of mind, enforcement can be taken too far. Such behavior is regularly replicated in society, for when people feel marginalized or powerless to control things in their lives, they often lash out in rage.

One event does not define a person, but in my mother's case, she suffered from a lifetime schizo-affective disorder. As readers of chapter 4 know, during Sissy's teenage years, my sister often felt insecure, trying hard to overcome being labeled crazy or schizophrenic. Given my upbringing and genetic disposition, as a teenager, I showed signs of depression, and as an adult, I too was diagnosed with clinical depression and mood disorder. In my thirties, after the birth of my third son, I was involved in three car accidents in three weeks, so I knew something was wrong. Depression was becoming a lifetime struggle.

After Mom was institutionalized, her marriage failed, and Sissy and I went to live with our paternal grandparents. While living with Grandma and Grandpa Brown in Hickory, Pennsylvania, Sissy and I joined a larger family that included two older children (Aunt Sally and Uncle John) and Great-Grandma Paskutis. Despite my parents' separation, Dad visited us nightly and put us to bed with a story, and this period remains one of the most enjoyable of my life. As was customary at this time, Sissy and I were given bottles of watered-down wine to help us sleep through the night. As three-year-olds, we likely had fears of insecurity, and my grandparents hoped this drink would help us cope. Soon thereafter, following her discharge from psychiatric care, Mom came to live with us, and that helped settle us down.

Around the age of five, Sissy and I moved ten miles away to the small town of Morgan to live with our maternal grandparents and our mother. Because Sissy and I had entered school at the age of four, we had completed kindergarten and part of first grade before moving to Morgan. Our home in Morgan proved quite a change from Hickory. Though we now had neighbors nearby, we missed the fields and forests surrounding our Hickory home.

Having had limited exposure to Black children in Hickory, in Morgan I recall walking with my sister and our nanny around the neighborhood and seeing a group of Black children surrounding a Black and white boy who were fighting. I immediately thought the white boy would win, until my nanny set me straight. "Let me tell you what's going to happen," she said. "The Black boy is going to win, and all the Black boys are then going to beat up the white boy. He's the one who will end up losing."

In third grade, Sissy and I kept getting called to the principal's office, and I didn't know why. As it turned out, Sissy was an equal-opportunity bully, for along with bullying white kids, she had been bullying some of the Black kids, but since she and I looked alike, I was being blamed as well, even though I was innocent. When I went to the principal and proclaimed my innocence, indicating that the Black children were also calling me racist names, she quickly realized she had no case and let me go. As I learned later, the Black children were not calling me racist names indiscriminately, but only because they confused me with my bullying sister.

In grammar school, Sissy and I would go to a nearby store for candy during recess. One day I told my friend Dina, "I'll go in and buy something for a quarter, and when Mrs. Gross isn't looking, we can fill our pockets with candy." As it turns out, Mrs. Gross was not fooled, and she caught us stealing. Unfortunately, while my white friends and I were allowed back in the store, Dina was not, because she was Black. In addition, I lost a friend, because she wasn't allowed to play with me after that.

Around that time I was bitten by a rabid cat. In our family we always welcomed stray cats, so one day, when I came upon a group of dogs chasing a cat, I came to its rescue. It was scared and running for its life, so I opened up the door to our garage to let it in, then quickly closed the door so the dogs couldn't follow. Feeling sorry for the cat, I went to pick it up, and when I did so, it bit me in the hand, clear through to the bone of my index finger. The next day my grandmother found the cat dead. Within a few weeks, complications occurred. I was taken to the hospital, given rabies shots, and diagnosed with osteomyelitis, a fungal or bacterial disease that causes the bone to disintegrate. The joint of my index finger was removed, and I received a six-week treatment for rabies.

Highly contagious, I was quarantined in Children's Hospital for two months. During that period, only my mother came to visit me, and I became isolated emotionally. My sister was not allowed to visit, and my dad only came once to gesture through the window. My mom became my hero, for though she had to protect herself by putting on a special suit, she came to see me every day, subjecting herself to the restrictive protocol. For three years I lived with a crooked index finger, before undergoing corrective surgery.

In elementary school, my sister was not only my closest friend, but one of my only friends. I looked to her as my guardian and protector. We were both competitive with others, but not with one another. I looked up to her, and was not aware of her bullying. Another problem, however, soon became apparent, for while in elementary school, and later, in junior high, Sissy and I were members of a stealing club. Consisting of five girls, we encouraged one another to excel in stealing. In fact, we got quite good at deception, to the point of creating a reward for "the best theft of the week." One time I won the title after successfully removing socks from a mannequin.

On another occasion, one of the girls stole dozens of pairs of underwear at a nearby mall, while another entered a dressing room, where she put new clothes underneath her regular clothes. Another time, my sister stole a mouse, which she tried to hide in her clothes but which jumped from one shoulder to the other as she exited the store. When we got home, we hid the mouse in our house, where it survived for several months. Occasionally, my mother caught us in our thefts, and we were forced to return the stolen goods. Thankfully, these pranks didn't last long, for this behavior came to an end by the age of eleven.

In middle school, I became uncomfortable around others. Although my sister describes me as popular at this time, I was a loner. In high school, I worked as a short-order cook at the local truck stop called Twigs. At my current height of five feet eleven inches, I quickly learned how to deal with the advances of older men. Despite my size, I was gentle and nonaggressive, so I relied on mental and verbal skills. When one customer tried to be suggestive sexually, I simply told him my grandmother was newly single but that even she might be too young for him. That simple comment silenced him. By high school, I hit my stride athletically and academically, and this helped improve my depressed mental state. I ran track with my sister and two other twins, joining them on relay teams, and this formed a winning combination. Sissy and I had been born in the same hospital as the other set of twins, and only one day apart.

I also joined my sister on the basketball team, where she was the star. Though I dated occasionally, on the whole my high school years were years of social isolation. Having a job and going to work became therapeutic, for it put me in a more positive frame of mind. By tenth grade, I began working at Dairy Delight, where I felt responsible and productive.

At home, Grandma Brinley was our moral compass, for she held Sissy and me to high standards—no smoking and drinking—likely so we might not end up like our grandfather, who was an alcoholic, or like our mother, who drank occasionally and lived a compromised lifestyle. Conforming outwardly, internally, I was running from anxiety by chasing comfort and security.

One day I invited friends to a party at our house, and beer was present, but since we weren't allowed to drink at home, we left and drank outside. When I drank, my depression left me temporarily calm and clear headed. Though I didn't know I was depressed, I was fearful of becoming schizophrenic like my mother. Sissy and I grew up surrounded by mental instability, but when one of my mom's therapists suggested help for us, Grandma Brinley refused, for she didn't want us to be labeled odd or screwy.

In high school, I was regularly sad, and as I discovered later, my depression was in part due to anxiety. I began having anxiety attacks whenever I watched Billy Graham on television. He often spoke about death, so one day I decided to accept Jesus, following Graham's guidelines for being saved. While I trace my religious conversion to this date, dedicating my life to Christ did not alleviate my anxiety, for whenever I watched Graham's telecast, I would curl up in a ball on the floor. When my grandmother asked what was wrong, I could only reply, "I'm really scared!" At such times, I found my grandmother's advice not to worry comforting, for, as she put it, "God will call you when He is ready." However, after my grandfather's death, my fears intensified. When I thought about him I began tensing up, dreading my own death. I felt anxious regularly, particularly when I was around people at the mall, for I felt absolute terror at the thought that eventually everyone would be dead. Such thoughts are not normal, certainly not for teenagers, but lacking professional help, I had to deal with them on my own. Unable to face my fears, I pushed them deeper inside. Later on, this anxiety influenced my relations with my children, often with disastrous results, for instead of helping them with their fears, I taught them to bury their anxiety as well.

During high school, I only drank occasionally, but when I got to college, alcohol was readily available, and I drank frequently. According to popular surveys, Washington & Jefferson College was considered one of the nation's top-ten party or drinking schools at this time, and Sissy and I added to that reputation. While we had separate friends and took different classes, Sissy and I roomed together and played on championship basketball teams together. I enjoyed my classes, majoring in English and minoring in Sociology in preparation for a career in social work.

Unfortunately, my highs were when I got drunk and my lows occurred when I was hung over. It was tragic to see classmates become alcoholics or institutionalized for drug addiction. Though fraternities frequently socialized with sororities, one fraternity, needing additional beer money, started a Little Sisters organization, which Sissy and I joined. As unaffiliated independents, the only expectation was that we chip in with beer money. In my senior year, I finally sobered up in preparation for graduation, and I attained my goal of making the Dean's List. Along the way, I took a couple of religion electives, and I found them awesome.

During college, Sissy and I worked for a housecleaning service. After graduation, we decided to start our own business, which we called Capital Cleaning Services. Around this time, Sissy and I joined a singles group called the Tall Peoples' Club, and as a fundraiser for this group we started a basketball tournament. A lady came to interview us regarding membership in the club, bringing with her a good-looking younger man named Ray Morrow. Ray and I hit it off at that interview and soon began dating. He was a doer and fixer, and not a talker, a hands-on, matter-of-fact guy, and I found that attractive.

Soon thereafter I became pregnant, and as a result, Ray and I decided to get married. Our marriage took place on May 17, 1986, and in November of that year our son Raymond Morrow III was born. Two years earlier, I had enlisted in the Army Reserves. I had been interested in law enforcement, and the Reserves seemed like a good way to gain experience while making money. In addition, the job was only occasional and part-time, which suited my schedule. I entered as an MP (Military Police), and upon completion I was hired by the State Police, but due to my pregnancy, I quit before I had a chance to begin.

After the birth of my son Ray, I also took a job with Aspen Systems, a legal data base, deciding that a career in social work would be too draining emotionally. For a while I worked both jobs simultaneously—Aspen Systems from 3 to 11 p.m. and Capital Cleaning during the day. One of the projects we researched at work involved the Love Canal, a neighborhood in Niagara Falls, New York infamous for a landfill that became the site of an environmental disaster in the 1970s, where decades of dumping toxic chemicals harmed the health of hundreds of residents.

I was working several jobs at the time, placing my son in daycare and getting family members to pitch in occasionally at night. There is no doubt that my addiction to work really hurt my family, but for me, work had become a place of refuge. One redemptive factor was that by this time I had quit drinking. In 1989, when our nation was experiencing an economic recession, my husband went to the San Francisco area of California in search of a job. He had a friend there and there was a need for construction workers. After Ray took a job, my son and I joined him. Shortly before I moved to California, my brother Jim brought his two-year-old son Matt to live with me and my son Ray, who was only a year older than Matt. Jim's wife, Sandy, had been institutionalized with psychotic postpartum depression while Jim was serving on a naval base in San Diego, so Jim brought Matt to live with me temporarily and newly-born Julia to live with Sissy. Thus, when I moved to California, Matt came with me.

Eventually, as readers might recall from Sissy's account, Jim and Sandy were divorced and Jim gained custody of his children, bringing them back to Pennsylvania upon his discharge from the Navy. In 1991, while I was still in California, my second son Maxwell Morrow was born. Around this time, I met three women at a community park. All three were committed Christians and they played an important role in my Christian growth. Each was active in her church, and I began attending various churches, at times with them and other times on my own. One of these ladies was a free spirit, an ecumenist who maintained no specific membership but visited many churches. Another was the wife of a youth pastor, so I often attended her church. The third attended church with her husband, and they participated together in Bible studies. My husband Ray attended his own church and occasionally joined me, but more out of obligation than out of devotion, for he regularly slept through the sermon.

Though I had grown up in church and felt I had always been a Christian, I had recommitted to Christ on several occasions, including as a child while watching Billy Graham rallies on television and then again with my California friends. A few years ago, Sissy and I took my grandson and all three of us were baptized at a local evangelical church, and this became another significant step in my faith journey. Shortly thereafter, Sissy and her husband Jim started their study group Body in Spirit, and I joined, participating occasionally in the discussions on spirituality and the Bible.

In 1996, our third son, Arthur, was born, and he came as a complete surprise. We thought he was an ovarian cyst. My marriage was going poorly, and when I discovered I was pregnant, Ray and I considered an abortion. However, on our way to the procedure, we changed our mind, and I am so grateful that I did.

My marriage continued for several additional years after that. In 1999, Ray and I returned from California, for living there had become too expensive. For a short time we were able to live with my sister and her fiancé Jim, until we were able to afford our own home. I was glad to be back with Sissy, whom I had missed terribly while in California.

Though I tried to be a good mother and wife, my part of the first marriage failed because I was insecure and self-centered. I was withdrawn and despondent. My husband began to give up on me, for I was not fun to live with. One day we purchased a camcorder, and when I saw myself on camera, I didn't like what I saw. I looked sad, and I couldn't seem to rid the lost look from my face. Unable to recognize myself and after seeking professional help, I came to see how aloof I had become.

I had never been treated for depression, and it was only after the birth of my third son that I began to address my mental state. In California I had wrecked three cars within two weeks, so my General Practitioner put me on Prozac, which helped me become more interactive and present in people's lives. After years of anxiety and depression, I immediately began feeling balanced and grounded.

Moving back to Pennsylvania, I began working as a personal aide at Asbury Place, an assisted living facility in nearby Mount Lebanon. starting at a lock-down unit for patients with memory impaired function. Over time I graduated to medical technician, doing much of the work performed by nurses. Because the job required careful attention to detail, I went on ADD (attention deficit disorder) medication. Because the medication got to be too expensive, I trained to become a Certified Nursing Assistant, which allowed me to practice in a more skilled unit and earn a better income.

I stayed at Asbury Place for ten years, and loved working there under a Christian staff.

In 2001, while separated from my husband but before my divorce, I moved in with my mother, living next door to Sissy and Jim. Mom had just completed a 28-day rehab program at Gateway, after which she quit drinking, and though she relapsed once after that, she remained sober for the rest of her life.

Shortly after the kids and I moved in with Mom, I began experiencing severe abdominal pains, eventually diagnosed as endometriosis, a disease in which the tissue that lines the inside of the uterus begins growing outside the uterus. Partly an autoimmune problem, in my case the cells of my intestines began growing abnormally. After two ineffective exploratory surgeries, a third surgery provided a correct diagnosis and removal of the harmful tissue.

Prior to my diagnosis, I was using an archaic heating pad to alleviate pain. One Saturday, when I was alone, I accidentally left the heating pad plugged in. Mom had gone away overnight to attend a program with Sissy and Jim, and my kids had been visiting with friends when I went to pick them up and take them to be with their dad. On the way to his house, I heard sirens going off, and when I returned home, I found my house had caught on fire and had partly burned. On the dining room table, in a part of the structure that still remained, I found the insurance application papers Mom and I had been filing out to apply for home insurance. The house, particularly the living room, where the fire had started, had suffered substantial damage—and we had no insurance! Among other things, the upright piano was incinerated, and the fire burned through the ceiling to the bedroom above.

As I learned later, a lady on the ridge across from my house had seen the smoke and called 911. Had it not been for her quick action, the entire house would have burned. Overwrought and alone, I felt I had run out of options. No one was next door, and I had just found our pets—three cats and a dog—dead inside, probably from smoke inhalation. Feeling lost and despondent, I went to Sissy's house next door to get my bearings.

While I was there, I heard a persistent knock on the door, and it was Zach, a kid from the neighborhood the same age as my middle son. He told me that his house had burned down once, and that he could understand my loss. Having overcome adversity, he had taken up a collection, and it was about ten dollars. Inviting him in, we ordered pizza with the money he had collected. After some small talk, he couldn't help asking, "You know, we're all wondering how the fire started." He knew that my mother was on a lot of meds, and he thought that possibly she had caused the fire.

"No," I replied, "My mother wasn't here. I left the heating pad plugged in the wall socket. It was very old and the wiring overheated. I caused the fire."

Helen's Personality and Spirituality Profile

Helen's MBTI results are INFP. Unlike Georgia's dominant function, which is "F," or Jim's dominant, which is "S," Helen's dominant function is "N." Described as Mediator, Helen is a person with Introverted, Intuitive, Feeling, and Perceiving personality traits. A rare personality type, Mediators tend to be quiet, open-minded, and imaginative, and they apply a caring and creative approach to everything they do.

Although they may seem quiet or unassuming, Mediators (INFPs) have vibrant, passionate inner lives. Creative and imaginative, they happily lose themselves in daydreams, inventing all sorts of stories and conversations in their minds. These personalities are known for their sensitivity—Mediators can have profound emotional responses to music, art, nature, and the people around them. Idealistic and empathetic, Mediators long for deep, soulful relationships, and they feel called to help others. However, because this personality type makes up such a small portion of the population, Mediators may sometimes feel lonely or invisible, adrift in a world that doesn't seem to appreciate the traits that make them unique.

Given these personality attributes and needs, coupled with the frequent disruptions and disappointments in her life, is it any wonder that Helen occasionally felt lonely and distraught? In times like these, she was regularly sustained by her faith in God's plan for her life, recognizing that goodness is better than perfection. Relying on God-given gifts, she has discovered in her exodus story a journey from bondage to freedom. Like Helen, we too can discover in the gospels a Jesus who, in dismissing certainties, shows us what freedom means, for this Jesus is always calling followers to leave the safety and security of their nets and follow him into newness of life.

Mediators share a sincere curiosity about the depths of human nature. Introspective to the core, they're exquisitely attuned to their own thoughts and feelings, but they yearn to understand the people around them as well. Mediators are compassionate and nonjudgmental, always willing to hear another person's story. When someone opens up to them or turns to them for comfort, they feel honored to listen and be of help. While empathy is one of this personality type's greatest gifts, it can be a liability at times. The troubles of the world weigh heavily on Mediators' shoulders, and these personalities can be vulnerable to internalizing other people's negative moods or mindsets. Unless they learn to set boundaries, Mediators may feel overwhelmed by just how many wrongs there are that need to be set right.

Few things make Mediators more uneasy than pretending to be someone they aren't. With their sensitivity and their commitment to authenticity, people with this personality type tend to crave opportunities for creative self-expression. It comes as no surprise, then, that many famous Mediators are poets, writers, actors, and artists. They can't help but muse about the meaning and purpose of life, dreaming up all sorts of stories, ideas, and possibilities along the way. Through these imaginative landscapes, Mediators can explore their own inner nature as well as their place in the world. While this is a beautiful trait, these personalities sometimes show a tendency to daydream and fantasize rather than take action. To avoid feeling frustrated, unfulfilled, or incapable, Mediators need to make sure that they take steps to turn their dreams and ideas into reality.

People with this personality type tend to feel directionless or stuck until they connect with a sense of purpose for their lives. For many Mediators, this purpose has something to do with uplifting others and their ability to feel other people's suffering as if it were their own. While Mediators want to help everyone, they need to focus their energy and efforts—otherwise, they can end up exhausted. Fortunately, Mediators are resilient, and their creativity and idealism can bloom even after the darkest of seasons. Although they know the world will never be perfect, Mediators still care about making it better however they can. This quiet belief in doing the right thing may explain why these personalities so often inspire compassion, kindness, and beauty wherever they go.

Empathic, generous, and open-minded, Mediators love to see things from unconventional perspectives. Passionate and idealistic, Mediators are ready to give their whole heart to an idea or movement that captures their imagination. People with this personality type may not always be outspoken, but they are consistent, striving to follow their conscience, even when doing the right thing isn't easy or convenient. They rarely lose sight of their desire to live a meaningful, purpose-filled life—one that helps others and leaves the world a better place.

Despite their wonderful strengths, Mediators are also beset by weaknesses such as self-isolation, lack of focus, idealistic and hopeless romanticism, emotional vulnerability, and lack of focus. Introspective to a fault and yearning for harmony and acceptance, they will avoid conflict as much as possible. Hence, unless they establish boundaries, they can be at risk of absorbing other people's negative moods or attitudes. When someone dislikes or disapproves of them, these personalities, desperate to please, may become fixated on trying to clear the air and change that person's mind. Unfortunately, this can drain their energy, eclipsing their inner wisdom and their awareness of their own needs. Believing in their unique potential, and desperately wanting to live up to it, Mediators can set unrealistic expectations for themselves. Taken too far, this self-criticism can discourage Mediators, leading them to give up on even their dearest dreams.

As dreamers and idealists, especially when it comes to romance, Mediators believe in the power and beauty of true love, and they sincerely hope never to settle for anything else. They don't just want to find a partner—they want to connect with a soul mate. Thoughtful and open-minded, these personalities are generally willing to consider going out with all sorts of people. Mediators pride themselves on their ability to look past a potential partner's superficial traits—such as appearance, social status, or possessions—and focus on deeper, more meaningful aspects of compatibility. On account of their idealism, it can be difficult—if not impossible—for a flesh-and-blood person to live up to a Mediator's cherished dreams. However, perseverance can lead to a great deal of joy when they find their soul mate.

Devoted and loyal, they nevertheless respect their partner's independence, aiming to accept their partners as they are. That said, these personalities also want to help their partners learn, grow, and pursue their goals. Mediators are always dreaming up ways to improve themselves and the world around them, and the last thing they'd want is for their partners to feel unhappy or stuck. Mediators tend to promote harmony over disagreement. Although this lends stability to their relationships, it can also lead to problems. To avoid triggering a conflict, Mediators may avoid talking openly about things that are bothering them—instead, they might mentally fixate on the problem or try to solve it on their own. They may also focus on making their partner happy, to the detriment of their own priorities and sense of self.

When it comes to their social lives, Mediators (INFPs) may find themselves caught in a web of contradictions. People with this personality type crave alone time, but they're also vulnerable to loneliness. They long to feel accepted and well-liked, but they hate the idea of pretending to be anyone but their authentic selves. And while they hesitate to draw attention to themselves, they don't want to be invisible, either. The good news is that, in the company of true friends, Mediators can escape their insecurities and focus on what really matters. For these personalities, friendship is a precious commodity—an opportunity for friends to lift each other uop and change each other's lives for the better. Perhaps because of their intense investment in these relationships, Mediators tend to feel most fulfilled by spending time with a small, intimate circle of friends. Acquaintances may come and go, but this inner circle is likely to include Mediators' friends for life. Though they don't always find it easy to make friends, Mediators are looking for lasting, authentic friendships with people who share their desire to think and feel deeply, to do the right thing, and to give more to the world than they take from it.

For Mediators, life is a journey, and they feel called to help other people embark on their own journeys toward meaning, fulfillment, and happiness. In their understated, nondomineering way, Mediators love guiding others to learn and grow. People with this personality type delight in their children's wide-eyed wonder at the world, and they want to give their children freedom—freedom to form their own opinions, discover their own interest, and grow into their unique selves. Thought they enjoy raising free spirits, this doesn't mean they are totally hands-off. They want to teach key values to their children, including honesty, compassion, and the importance of caring for others. They also want their children to understand the meaning of personal responsibility, especially when it comes to not hurting others.

Few personality types are as poetic and kindhearted as INFPs. With their unique gifts, Mediators can overcome all sorts of challenges and obstacles—and brighten the lives of those around them in the process. Yet Mediators can be tripped up in areas where idealism and altruism are more of a liability than an asset. When it comes to finding (or keeping) a partner, making friends, pursuing a meaningful career, or planning for the future, people with this personality type may need to consciously develop their weaker traits and gain new skills—even as they draw on their many strengths.

Typed on the Enneagram as a Type Five (dominant) with a Six "wing" (auxiliary), Helen is also an Investigator or Observer. Type Fives are alert, insightful, and curious. Their primary virtue is *Detachment*. They are able to concentrate and focus on developing complex ideas and skills. Independent and innovative, they can become preoccupied with their thoughts and imaginary constructs. They become detached, yet high-strung and intense. They typically have problems with isolation, eccentricity, and nihilism. Their primary Passion is *Avarice*. At their best, healthy Fives are visionary pioneers, often ahead of their time and able to see the world in an entirely new way. Type Sixes, also known as Loyalists or Critics, are reliable, hardworking, and responsible, but they can also be defensive, evasive, and highly anxious—running on stress while complaining about it. Their primary virtue is *Courage*. They are often cautious and indecisive but can also be reactive, defiant, and rebellious. They typically have problems with self-doubt and suspicion. Their primary Passion is *Fear* or anxiety about possible future events. At their best, healthy Sixes are internally stable, self-confident, and self-reliant, courageously supporting the weak and powerless.

As an INFP, Helen's spirituality type is an "NF." As noted in Georgia's profile,

> NFs are characterized by a *questing spirituality*. NF youth like to please the adults and peers in their lives. They can be easily crushed by disapproval or even indifference. They need regular affirmation from parents and teachers if their self-esteem and self-image are not to suffer. Because they see possibilities in the future (N) and like to gain approval from others, they often will prepare for careers and causes in response to adult mentors in their lives. NF youth are exceedingly idealistic. Their idealism is often unpredictable; some young men may overcompensate for their F by expressing their idealism in hostile ways. They are strongly represented among protestors for social issues. NF adults are enthusiastic and insightful, recognizing the personal needs of others. Idealists by nature, they always see a way to make life better. They have an ability to draw people into a discussion and to facilitate consensus-building for social harmony and good. NFs on a healthy track will regularly draw others toward their own best selves. The Intuitive proclivity for symbol and metaphor, combining with global vision for the well-being of the world, makes NFs inspired communicators of the ideal. Future-oriented and attuned to the big picture of life as a whole, NFs tend to focus more on possibilities than on concrete situations at hand. Their N nature is balanced, however, by their F side,

> which keeps them in touch with reality and keeps their utopian bent in check. Flexible and open to change, NFs see life as continual self-creating process, a quest toward selfhood. Their malleable natures exist to be formed and re-formed in ever more exquisite patterns of self-actualization. NFs seek increasing meaning and spiritual purpose in life.

Combining Urban Holmes' Spirituality Wheel and John Westerhoff's approach, as an "N," Helen's spiritual typological preference is Type III: affective-apophatic or mystical. This type, which emphasizes being and direct experience of God, is called "mystical" because its primary aim is union with the Holy, an unattainable goal, yet a journey that nevertheless continually impels seekers onward.

8

Bob's Story

Although I enjoy working quietly and independently, I am a reliable team player, for I like to solve problems. Though things come naturally to me, I don't spend much time speculating and theorizing, and I don't consider myself an abstract thinker. I am what might be called a practical thinker, for I am a doer and a fixer. Having been raised on a farm in Idaho, I am a hands-on person. Following my spontaneous nature, I like playing things by ear and going with the flow. However, when I make plans, I like them to go perfectly, and that's rarely possible.

My spirituality, like my life, is private, personal, and unique. While I believe in a higher power, I find little comfort in doctrine or theology. As a child, I attended Sunday School and church regularly, but on the whole I found the weekly services confining, repetitive, and boring. My siblings and I were required to attend, an obligation I found distinctly unappealing. I failed to see how people could experience God socially or in indoor settings. I wished to be free to experience truth and reality practically, not abstractly or theoretically, and I preferred the freedom of the great outdoors to the confinement of church worship.

When it comes to organized religion, I find many people are hypocritical in their practice, proclaiming beliefs and ideals they rarely practice or limit to one day of the week. My experience with certain Christian sects or denominations is that their members are quick to condemn the beliefs and behaviors of others while rarely finding fault with themselves. Good dualists, they see only black or white or right and wrong. And, of course, they claim to be right, while those who disagree are viewed as categorically wrong. Such people often appear to me to be closed to anything new or different, unable to see gradations in truth or theology. Thankfully, not all believers are like that, for some are quite tolerant, but most of the organized religion I've run across seems to have a "my way or the highway" mindset.

In school, I found most teachers dull and uninteresting, often speaking in monotone or lacking enthusiasm for their subject matter. Despite completing twelve years of required public education, I consider myself self-taught. To some extent, that holds true for most of my siblings; we are all "pig-headed" and bear the Benson mentality. Like many of my ancestors, I never pursued a college education, though like many Depression-era folks, I feel I earned a degree in the "college of hard-knocks."

Exposed to the Bible at an early age, I still read it occasionally, particularly in family settings with my wife, but I find many of its teachings contradictory or irrelevant. As I see it, Bible reading requires a process of filling in the blanks. While much of the Bible is unclear, deliberately so, I believe it is up to us to complete its message by making it clear, applying it in our own way.

While many people relate to God through prayer, whether verbally or silently, that is not my approach. Unlike most religious folks, who pray when they feel desperate or insecure, I see prayer more as an act of reverence than desperation. Moreover, I don't believe in asking God for benefits or for help due to negligence or distress. What is the point in using God as an excuse for our own failure or weakness when God expects mature believers to be responsible and resourceful adults?

Although I value the company of family and friends, I enjoy silence. Throughout my life I have felt most balanced and in harmony with myself, nature, and my higher power when running freely through forests and fields and along rivers and streams. That feeling of unity and wellness also occurs whenever I can be of help to others, like when I help my wife in her garden, and how I feel at peace while riding back roads on my motorcycle.

While I don't have insightful stories about my ancestors, I know that my forebears where in this country for many generations. My paternal ancestors were Scandinavian, and my maternal ancestors were English. My great-grandfather James Benson and his wife Maggie lived in Deep Creek, Wyoming, a small town no longer in existence, where James ran a country store and Maggie was the postmistress. One of my sisters possesses a log book with records of transactions at my great-grandfather's store, which record what people purchased and how much they owed. These records are also coded, to indicate whether account owners were cattlemen or sheepherders. A phenomenon at that time, known as "sheep wars," involved armed conflict between sheepmen and cattlemen over grazing rights. These conflicts were most common in Texas, Arizona, and the border region of Wyoming and Colorado. For their own protection and financial survival, small business owners needed to know on which side customers stood.

At some point the family moved to Moscow, Idaho. Of the three sons that survived, two moved to Seattle, one to work in the shipyards and the other to work for Boeing aircraft. Both were naturally gifted in technical and mechanical skills. Land was plentiful around 1900, and the third son (my grandfather), also named James, married a local gal named Ida Belle and purchased a sizeable farm of 530 acres. My father, James E. Benson (1931–2023), an only child who went by his middle name Edd, grew up on that farm and began working in a body and fender shop before returning to the farm in 1968, at his father's death. While he owned some livestock, he mostly grew crops such as wheat, barley, peas, and lentils. Realizing that there was little money to be made in farming, Dad sold the farm equipment and put the land up for lease. For I while, I helped with chores, working for the person who leased the farm, while Dad started a household repair business. My grandad always dreamed of developing a mobile trailer park, but it was my dad who turned that vision into reality, doing most of the work himself. Eventually he created a thirty- to forty-mobile house court on our farm property, which he then rented to residents.

When my dad met and married Sally Anne Parks (1935–1997), her father was a barber in the nearby town of Troy. In 1968, when my parents went to live on the farm, I was seven years old, and I had two older sisters and a younger twin brother and sister. As children, we played outdoors, climbing nearby hills, fishing on our pond, and in the spring, playing in the run-off streams that flowed freely from melted snow and heavy spring rains. I always had neighbors and close friends, many of them living in the trailer park nearby.

On the whole, I found school dull and boring, for many of the subjects came easily to me, and I found other subjects uninteresting, so I didn't accelerate through them as I might had I taken an interest. While I read occasionally, I was more mechanically oriented and always enjoyed working with my hands. In addition to putting plastic models together, at an early age I learned to drive farm and motor vehicles, regularly volunteering to plow snow with our tractor. In Idaho, the age limit for driving is fourteen, so soon thereafter, having completed Drivers Education class, I began driving the family car.

I moved through grammar school, junior high, and high school automatically and without incident. During my childhood, I had one very close friend, but as a teenager, that number grew to three. We began riding motorcycles, and became adept at making our own repairs. In high school, I completed my required courses early on, and was able to coast through my junior and senior years with hands-on courses such as woodshop. Mathematics had always come easy to me, so that when I was in eleventh grade, I became a student aide, helping teach math to seniors.

By 1979, when I graduated from high school, I had no occupation in mind, so I went to work at a grocery store. That work continued for the next four or five years, but only as a backup plan. At the time, my brother-in-law Arthur was a career non-commissioned officer in the Air Force. A longtime friend, he helped me make a decision, and in 1984 I enlisted in the Air Force as well, stationed for ten years both in the United States and in England. A few years earlier, while visiting Arthur at his home, I had finally taken notice of his younger sister Amanda, who had been a year behind us in school. I liked her spirit and her demeanor, and when she came with us guys four-wheeling on our jeeps, we bonded, and that led to our marriage in 1982.

During my decade in the Air Force, I served on four different bases, beginning at Clovis AFB in New Mexico, where my daughter Melissa was born. When I got an assignment overseas, I couldn't take Amanda unless I reenlisted, so that's what I did. In England, I served a four-year stint at RAF Lakenheath, working on F–111 and B–1B bombers as an avionic tech. While in England, our second daughter Heather was born.

Amanda and I thoroughly enjoyed our experience overseas, although there were times of culture shock. One example occurred when we looked at a house to discover that central heating was not whole-house heating but a stove in the middle of the house that only partly reached the bedroom and bath. Also, when we were invited to visit the owner of our bungalow, we saw a commemorative plaque on the wall, which contained an engraved invitation to tea given by the Queen. Although the tea included some one hundred guests, such invitations were highly cherished and viewed as a highlight for British commoners.

After serving in England, my family returned with me to the United States, where I continued performing tech work at Plattsburgh AFB in upstate New York, and when that base closed, I was transferred to Ellsworth AFB in South Dakota. In the 1990s, the military enacted a program of forced reduction and I accepted severance and release from duty. While serving on base in South Dakota, I learned that Amanda had been unfaithful. I felt blindsided, because I had no idea this was happening. Thus, it became clear that our marriage was over. We separated and divorced quickly in 1994, at which time I took retirement from the Air Force and returned home to Idaho, where I took a job in electrical sales. According to our divorce agreement, Amanda had custody of the girls during the school year, and I had custody during the summer.

Soon thereafter Amanda remarried, this time to Richard Bauer, a member of the Jehovah's Witnesses, with whom she had a child. As is the practice among the JWs, holidays and birthdays are not to be celebrated. Not long after, Amanda called to inform me that Melissa no longer wished to live with her stepfather and requested that I take her. I did so, bringing her back home with me to Idaho, and that year, while in school, Melissa had a meltdown, and that's when I learned that she had been molested by her stepfather. Melissa not only lamented having been sexually abused, but feared that Heather was also vulnerable. At that point, youth services in South Dakota were informed, and Richard was forced to leave the residence while Heather was there. Eventually, with my support, Melissa took her stepfather to court where, during his trial, he was charged with seventy-six counts of sexual misconduct. He was then sentenced to an extended term in jail, not to end before his child with Amanda was eighteen years old.

While living in Idaho, I became acquainted with Ann, who was doing postdoctoral work at Washington State University, but when she moved to Boston, I wasn't able to move with her. Looking for a companion, I found a match on an online dating service with Diana, who lived in Bellwood, near Altoona, Pennsylvania. Ready to take a risk, I took Melissa and went to live with Diana, only to experience almost immediate disappointment with my match. However, anxious to make it work, I stayed with Diana for some eight years. Over time, I found my unhappiness with Diana and her controlling nature spilling over to my relationship with my daughters, particularly with Melissa. I felt angry much of the time, and no matter what I did, it never seemed good enough. For a time, my relationship with Melissa became so strained and conflicted that I felt compelled to place her in foster care, where she finished high school.

After high school, Melissa enlisted in the Marines, but after being diagnosed with fibromyalgia, a disorder known to cause fatigue, loss of sleep, and a heightened sensitivity to pain, she received a discharge. Eventually she met Ray Ronk, and after living with him for a while, she became pregnant. At the time I had bought a house in Altoona and had a secure job working with Scott Electric.

While I was living with Diana, Heather came to visit us one summer, and when Diana suggested that we keep her with us and enroll her in school, I agreed. When I called the judge charged with Heather's case, I received temporary custody, and Amanda decided not to contest the decision. A few years later, after Heather graduated from high school, she began attending a local branch of Penn State University. Then, after a brief marriage, she moved into a lasting relationship with her current boyfriend.

Unable to extricate myself from my explosive relationship with Diana, I took two jobs. Living in her duplex for a while, we eventually moved into our own house, but after hearing her say how she missed her old apartment, and learning that it was available for rent, I persuaded her to return without me. After Diana left, I sold our house and moved into a duplex in Bellwood. Looking across the street one day, I noticed a lady on her front porch with two dogs. One was an Australian cattle dog, so intrigued, I decided to meet my neighbor and get acquainted with her dogs. As we talked, I learned her name was Kate, and that she was a Physician Assistant. Over time, we established a friendship, one of the strongest I ever had. Despite learning that she was gay, our friendship grew.

As friends, we occasionally socialized and ate out together, but her favorite recreational activity was trail running. One day I hinted I might join her, but she brushed me off, indicating I might not enjoy it. Then one morning she showed up at my apartment, knocked on the door, and handed me a pair of running shoes.

"Go ahead and put them on," she said, "and let's go for a run." That run turned into an obsession, for I began running about forty miles a week with her, sometimes twice a day, once in the morning and again that evening. On weekends we did our "marathon runs," spending hours running through the woods. On those occasions, we didn't follow trails, but across creeks and through the brush. We always wore good running shoes with excellent ankle support, and never got seriously injured. Over time, Kate and I started moving in different circles. Today, she is in Arizona, and we have gone our own ways.

Bob's Personality and Spirituality Profile

Bob's MBTI results are ISTP. Unlike Georgia's dominant function, which is "F," Jim's dominant, which is "S," or Helen's dominant function, which is "N," Bob's dominant function is "T." Described as Virtuoso, Bob is a person with Introverted, Sensing, Thinking, and Perceiving personality traits. Virtuosos tend to have an individualistic mindset, pursuing goals without needing much external connection. They engage in life with inquisitiveness and personal skill, varying their approach as needed.

Virtuosos love to explore with their hands and their eyes, touching and examining the world around them with cool rationalism and spirited curiosity. People with this personality type are natural makers, moving from project to project, building the useful and the superfluous for the fun of it, and learning from their environment as they go. Often mechanics and engineers, Virtuosos find no greater joy than in getting their hands dirty pulling things apart and putting them back together, just a little bit better than they were before.

ISTPs explore ideas through creating, troubleshooting, trial and error, and first-hand experience. They enjoy having other people take an interest in their projects and sometimes don't even mind them getting into their space. Of course, that's on the condition that those people don't interfere with their principles and freedom, and if others want to pursue a relationship with them, they will need to be open to Virtuosos returning the interest in kind. Virtuosos enjoy lending a hand and sharing their experience, especially with the people they care about, and it's a shame they're so uncommon, making up only about five percent of the population.

While their mechanical tendencies can make them appear simple at a glance, Virtuosos are actually quite enigmatic. Friendly but very private, calm but suddenly spontaneous, extremely curious but unable to stay focused on formal studies, Virtuoso personalities can be a challenge to predict, even by their friends and loved ones. Virtuosos can seem very loyal and steady for a while, but they tend to build up a store of impulsive energy that explodes without warning, taking their interests in bold new directions. Virtuosos' decisions stem from a sense of practical realism, and at their heart is a strong sense of direct fairness. The biggest issue ISTPs are likely to face is that they often act too soon, taking for granted their permissive nature and assuming that others are the same. Those who lack knowledge or appreciation for this time may be confused when Virtuosos suddenly change their plans because something more interesting came up.

Understanding Bob's personality and his aversion to jumping through other people's hoops, it become clear why he never wished to go to college. He could have excelled academically in college, but favoring working practically with his hands over theorizing with his brain, he probably would have been bored with all the cookie-cutter courses in return for a boatload of student debt.

People with the Virtuoso personality type struggle with boundaries and guidelines, preferring the freedom to move about and color outside the lines if they need to. Perhaps for this reason, Virtuosos have a particular difficulty in predicting emotions, but this is just a natural extension of their fairness as well as their tendency to explore their relationships through their actions rather than through empathy.

Optimistic and energetic, creative and practical, spontaneous and rational, virtuosos are naturals in crisis situations. People with this personality type usually enjoy taking risks, and they aren't afraid to get their hands dirty when the situation calls for it. Through all this, Virtuosos are able to stay quite relaxed. They live in the moment, refusing to worry too much about the future. Despite these strengths, Virtuosos are known to be stubborn, insensitive, private, and reserved. They are true introverts, keeping their personal matters to themselves, and often just prefer silence to small talk. Virtuosos enjoy novelty, which makes them excellent tinkerers, but much less reliable when it comes to focusing on things long-term. Once something is understood, Virtuosos tend to simply move on to something new and more interesting. Virtuosos thrive on diversity and unpredictability. Born problem solvers, no other type is quite as fascinated by how things work, how tools can be used, and how facts can be put together to create immediate and satisfying results.

When it comes to romantic relationships, Virtuosos are a bit like Jell-O, alternating coldness and detachment with passion, spontaneity, and enjoyment of the moment. Nothing can be forced in Virtuoso relationships, but as long as they are given the space they need to be themselves, they will gladly enjoy the comforts of a steady partner for a lifetime. However, if a potential partner doesn't measure up, Virtuosos have no real problem walking away.

With their well-rounded and interesting array of hobbies, people with the Virtuoso personality type have no trouble making acquaintances, but when it comes to long-lasting friendships, they only relate to the few who they feel truly understand them. Much of this comes down to Virtuosos simply not wanting to be bound to any particular person or activity, and this can certainly impact their views and relationships to organized religion. While living in the present and enjoying whatever life brings, they are always free to do their own thing, following their motto "everything can be changed." Forcing virtuosos to commit to scheduled activities is probably the quickest way to end these friendships.

Virtuosos' interests are quite diverse, and they rarely have trouble coming up with exciting things to do. People with this personality type are talented when it comes to using their senses, and usually enjoy a little competition. This makes their hobbies, especially the more physical activities like fishing and crafts, particularly enjoyable with little company on the side. Virtuoso personalities are also thoughtful, rational people. Being fairly creative individuals themselves, they often enjoy discussing new ideas, but in the end, the point of sharing those ideas needs to be to take action. Dreaming is well and good, but talk is cheap, and discussions on abstract topics can only hold Virtuosos' attention so long before they decide to shift their focus to something they can do.

When it comes to parenting, Virtuosos give their children more freedom and opportunity to do whatever they want, within sensible limits of course, than any other personality type. It's a big world out there, meant to be explored and experienced. Nothing is quite as perplexing to Virtuoso parents as their children sitting inside and watching television all day. Relaxed, open-minded and flexible, Virtuoso personalities expect their children to use their freedom wisely—that is, to exploit it in the name of exploration and experience. Where Virtuoso parents struggle most, as with their other relationships, is in emotional bonding. Emotional control is something that children learn and adapt to over years, and comparatively unemotional Virtuosos are often left at a loss for what to do in the meantime. Virtuosos may just need to rely on a more able partner. Otherwise, it takes a great deal of conscious effort on their part to be able to provide the sort of emotional understanding and support their children need.

Few personality types are as bold and practical as Virtuosos. Known for their technical mastery and willingness to improvise, Virtuosos are good at finding unique solutions to seemingly impossible challenges. Virtuosos' desire to explore and learn new things is invaluable in many areas, including their own personal growth.

Typed on the Enneagram as a Type Five (dominant) with a Six "wing" (auxiliary), Bob, like Helen, is an Investigator or Observer. Type Fives are alert, insightful, and curious. Their primary virtue is *Detachment*. They are able to concentrate and focus on developing complex ideas and skills. Independent and innovative, they can become preoccupied with their thoughts and imaginary constructs. They become detached, yet high-strung and intense. They typically have problems with isolation, eccentricity, and nihilism. Their primary Passion is *Avarice*. At their best, healthy Fives are visionary pioneers, often ahead of their time and able to see the world in an entirely new way. Type Sixes, also known as Loyalists or Critics, are reliable, hardworking, and responsible, but they can also be defensive, evasive, and highly anxious—running on stress while complaining about it. Their primary virtue is *Courage*. They are often cautious and indecisive but can also be reactive, defiant, and rebellious. They typically have problems with self-doubt and suspicion. Their primary Passion is *Fear* or anxiety about possible future events. At their best, healthy Sixes are internally stable, self-confident, and self-reliant, courageously supporting the weak and powerless.

As an ISTP, Bob's spirituality type is "ST." As noted in chapter 2,

> STs are characterized by a *task-oriented spirituality*. ST youth are drawn to activities that are task-oriented, such as team sports. And often they will be leaders. They learn by experience, wanting to discover things for themselves; they need to know why things are required and how they work. As teens STs divide into two groups: the freedom lovers (STPs) and the responsible ones (STJs), but all are oriented around well-defined institutions. When they grow up, STs become the realists, always in touch with the facts, unbiased, objective, accurate, paying attention to relevant details. They are skilled administrators, responsible, consistent, efficient, and analytical.
>
> STs commit themselves to the building up and maintaining of institutions, reliably and loyally. They prefer direct, experience-based, often physical activities, working with their hands or otherwise directly in situations, trying out procedures to see what works best, often preferring technical tasks to those requiring people skills. They learn best on the job, noticing relevant details, collecting facts, and verifying them directly by the senses. They arrive at conclusions in a linear cause-and-effect way. Their opinions, based on their experience, will often be firmly held and based on common sense. A confusion of beliefs is intolerable for STs. They like to find

> a world in balance, with reliable structures that lead them toward the right way to go. For the Journey of Works, order and a clear message are essential conditions. Appreciating clear beliefs and reliable structure, they tend to be literalists and legalists in religion; commitment provides religion stability.

Combining Urban Holmes' Spirituality Wheel and John Westerhoff's approach, as a "T," Bob's spiritual typological preference is Type IV: speculative-apophatic or "apostolic." This type, a visionary, almost crusading type of spirituality, is called "apostolic" because its primary aim is to obey God's will completely. Its major concerns are witness to God's reign and striving for justice and peace.

9

Life Together

Helen and Bob's Story

Helen's Perspective

THE YEARS 2000 TO 2015 were the most challenging of my life. I can't say they were my low point, but they were life changing, and it all started with my endometriosis and the fire in my mom's house. In 2001, my divorce was finalized, and Ray and I shared custody of our children until my youngest son Arthur chose to join him. After my divorce, I went through several jobs before relocating to Altoona, Pennsylvania. In addition to having my thyroid removed during this period, I returned to Morgan to take care of my ailing mother, who died in 2015. On the plus side, in 2012 and 2013 I met and married Bob Benson, and we have been happily married for the past decade.

After the home fire of 2001, my longtime friend and former coworker Lenny came to the rescue. I began dating him after my divorce, and he had become quite attached to my children, taking them fishing and on day trips. Knowing of my misfortune with the house and my divorce, one day he came to see me with a ring in hand, prepared to propose marriage. I accepted, for I felt I was in love and ready for marriage yet again. He was about fifteen years older than I and was clearly ready to settle down. He offered to buy my mother's house, now uninhabitable, and gave a significant amount for the property while offering to pay to rebuild the house. Due to legal complications, the deed was placed in my name only, and Lenny's name was left out. Due to this error, eventually I went to the courthouse and paid the fee to add Lenny's name to the deed, and the deed remains in both our names. After paying the rebuilding costs, Lenny backed out of our engagement and left me to live in the house.

In need of a more secure income, I received training as a Certified Nurses Assistant and went to work in the longtime care unit of Masonic Village in Sewickley, Pennsylvania. After two years, I was fired for insubordination. This was the first time I had been fired, and it was because I had offended a patient's disruptive family member. Having my own vegetable garden, I loved growing things, so for a while I worked in a farmer's market, then in the produce department of several supermarkets. At one point, I also worked at Serenity Pines, a personal care home in nearby Bridgeville, where spirituality was valued and could be freely shared with patients and coworkers.

When I was forty-eight, I enrolled in an online dating service, where I met Bob Benson. His profile was the most down-to-earth, unpretentious profile I had ever seen, and I was immediately interested. The picture he had posted showed him in a worn-out T-shirt, and the picture looked like a selfie. Bob was living in Altoona, Pennsylvania, about one hundred miles east of Pittsburgh. He and I talked on the phone for a year, speaking freely about the ups and downs of our lives, our children, and our experience in the military. Bob's two daughters, Melissa and Heather, had been living with him when we began our relationship, but had recently moved out. Melissa had served in the Marines but was back and living on her own, and Heather had completed high school and had moved in with her older sister. Things seemed to be going fine for Bob; he had a steady job working as an electrician, but he was lonely.

After two years of visitation, I decided to move to Altoona to be with him. I found a job with Valley View Nursing Home, first as a nurse's aide, then as a supervisor. When a vacancy occurred at the county home, I applied, but my friends advised against it, telling me I couldn't do better than my current supervising job. However, I wanted a tough job, for I felt I needed hard physical labor to survive; direct, hands-on work with patients, not passive administrative work. I was pleased to get Bob's support for my decision. As we were both ready for a stable relationship, we agreed to get married.

I found Bob not only physically attractive and trustworthy but also supportive emotionally. Like myself, he was a doer. We had both survived disappointments in previous marriages, and the shared qualities and experiences provided a solid foundation for our relationship. We picked a date and were married privately by a Justice of the Peace. It was a second marriage for each of us, but it proved to be lasting.

In 2015, my mom got sick, so I took temporary leave at work and traveled back and forth to western Pennsylvania to care for her. Thinking she would survive her illness, Bob and I decided to move to Morgan. My home was vacant and Bob learned he could continue working for a local Scott Electric affiliate. In 2016, after Mom died, I found part-time work taking care of Joyce, an elderly lady with multiple sclerosis, giving her husband Sam relief to oversee his health-care business. Sissy had known this family, having cleaned their home through her housecleaning business. Thus, when Joyce's healthcare worker died, Sissy gave her my name, and I was able to step in. In 2022, I developed osteoarthritis in my knee that required knee replacement, and my doctor told me I couldn't continue to do the lifting required in caring for Joyce, so I was forced to quit that job. Having undergone one knee replacement, I am now convalescing from a second knee replacement, expecting to become mobile and fully functioning once again.

As I examine my life spiritually, I find that my spirituality serves as a daily foundation for all the fluctuations around and within me. Some days my spirituality seems richer and other times weaker and less vital, but I am confident that the period from 2000 to 2015—my most trying years—drew me closer to God.

As I think back to this period, despite the heartbreak and challenges, I see it as a time of spiritual growth and freedom, for from a spiritual perspective, I embrace these years as the dearest of my life, dearest because I came through agony to peace and fulfillment. However, when I become comfortable or complacent, I feel less desperate for God, and when I am lazy, I am farthest removed from God.

While I may not have attended church regularly between 2000 and 2015, I always had a support group, both nearby with Sissy and Jim but also at work. Providentially, my therapist was a Christian, as was my psychiatrist, whose husband served as a priest in the Eastern Orthodox Church. While providing caregiving service in the Pittsburgh and Altoona areas, it became clear to me that effective caregiving requires love and compassion grounded in faith and spirituality. As I can attest, sharing my faith with patients, sometimes verbally but primarily through my actions, helped me get through difficult times. And this became a two-way street, for whenever I shared my faith and trust in God with others, they did so with me. In my experience, miracles occur regularly in nursing homes, largely because the climate is supportive of faith and spirituality. On one occasion, one of the residents at Serenity Hills began leaving money anonymously at a local church, and the church members, guessing on the source, came to our nursing home and began a Bible study primarily for him.

Having seen the negative side of organized religion, I do not attend church regularly, though I do enjoy attending churches that focus on celebration and service over recruitment and dogma. As opposed to church activities, I find my spiritual needs best met through ecumenical and non-dogmatic friendships, small-group studies such as Sissy and Jim's Body in Spirit, but primarily through personal prayer, reading, journaling, and Bible study. As I discover in John 4:23–24, God blesses those who worship "in spirit and truth," and it is a personal form of spirituality that I find most fulfilling.

My husband's spirituality is different from mine, for he does not convey his beliefs and values verbally. If asked to describe Bob's spirituality, I would say it is deeply personal, internal, and wordless. He believes in a higher power, but leaves it at that. Although he is highly moral and deeply principled, religious creeds, dogmas, and sectarian denominations have little if any influence on his thinking and living. Body in Spirit, the group mentored by Dr. Vande Kappelle, helps me to be more tolerant of other people's spirituality, encouraging me to see spirituality in places and people not always evident or appreciated by those whose faith is more narrowly based or focused.

The glue in my relationship with Bob is that we are both doers and enjoy working on projects together, whether improving things around the house or making gardening easier or more successful. In this regard, Bob is always coming up with ideas that help make me happier and more efficient. One of my best personal qualities is my adaptability. I have come to see that things don't always need to be done my way, and I often find myself thinking of "we"—what makes things better or happier for our marriage—rather than solely about "me."

It helps that Bob is also adaptable, particularly regarding practical projects. He is very understanding, and things don't always have to be his way. He is also very patient; he rarely has preconceived ideas of how things should be, for he views every situation as unique. God has given me a great partner in Bob, and I find our personal qualities align to create effective teamwork. Since we are both introverts, we enjoy spending time together or just having the other nearby, even if this time is shared quietly. Like me, Bob can be moody, and we have learned to respect each other's need for privacy. Unlike Bob, who types as "T" on the Myers-Briggs typology, people like me, who type as "Fs," often have greater need for the company of others. Those who enter marriage often think they will be able to change aspects of their mates' behavior, but understanding personality theory lets us know how futile and even dangerous personality manipulation can be.

Knowing the futility of trying to change someone else's behavior, I have discovered that the interviewing process for this book, including learning about our personalities, has produced noticeable changes in my husband—including developing the self-awareness and openness required in telling his story—as well as a transformative effect on my relationship with Sissy. As a result, she and I are becoming more patient and understanding with one another, a breakthrough I find hopeful.

Bob's Perspective

I see life as a grand adventure. To undertake this venture, I need a home base. For me, that home base is a responsible relationship with my children and grandchildren and a lasting relationship with a spouse. When Melissa told me that she had become pregnant, I felt proud and honored but also fulfilled in life, for there was nothing more that I needed to do. I had never expected Melissa would become a mother, and now, having completed my first half of life, I began transitioning to my second half of life, embracing new hopes and opening myself to new possibilities. Now, after the birth of Melissa's third child, my sense of fulfillment has expanded to a sense of purpose, not only for my ongoing life but also in support of my children and grandchildren.

In 2007, while living in Altoona as a single parent, I became lonely once again. Desirous of female companionship, I signed up for an online dating service once again, looking not primarily for a spouse but for a significant new relationship. I had been betrayed once and mismatched a second time, but I was cautiously hopeful.

Learning I had matched well with a divorced lady in western Pennsylvania named Helen, I had mixed feelings, in part because she was living 112 miles away, and I had restricted my search to a 50-mile radius. After several emails and telephone conversations with her, I received notification from the dating service to call her, and that's when I began sensing that we were destined for more than friendship. Helen's dating profile had not posted her picture, but undeterred by that setback, I arranged to visit her in her home in the tiny town of Morgan. At the time, Helen was living with her second son Max, for her eldest son Ray was living on his own and Arthur, Helen's youngest, was living with his dad. In preparation for our visit, Helen sent Max to stay with a friend so we could spent a weekend alone. Things went well that weekend, and I felt our relationship could go in a good direction. It quickly became clear to me that Helen and I were destined to be together. Our interests aligned, and it seemed we were a perfect match.[1]

For several years Helen and I visited one another, and our relationship progressed evenly in mind, body, and spirit. Since I had a stable job, Helen decided to move in with me in Altoona, and in 2013, after a year of living together, we decided to get married. Having both been married previously, we decided on a small civil wedding. In 2015, Helen returned to western Pennsylvania to care for her ailing mother, and when I learned Scott Electric had started a franchise in the Pittsburgh area, I transferred there so Helen and I could live together in her Morgan home.

While there are multiple events or situations I consider high points in my relationship with Helen, I feel that the overarching reality in our marriage is our five children, my two girls and Helen's three boys, and their children. While I was not present when Helen's grandson Tyler was born, I was present at the birth of her other grandchildren as well as my three grandchildren. Thus, whether or not the offspring is biologically mine, they are our heritage, our blessing, and the highlight of our relationship.

Despite being stubborn, which I view as an extension of my reliability and dependability I am able to identify problems and fix them. In this respect, I see myself as reliable and tenacious, because to fix things one cannot be a quitter. At work, my boss knows he can count on me to show up regularly and punctually, and that makes me dependable. I hold myself to high standards, and I suppose I hold others to those same standards. While this was particularly true in the past, I feel I have become more tolerant and less perfectionistic over time. Though I am still stubborn and still get angry when others let me down, I feel my temperament is now more controlled.

One of Helen's best personal qualities is the effort she puts into pleasing others. She doesn't wish to disappoint, and that makes her a great caregiver, although this comes at a cost, particularly when her care of others is not reciprocated. With Helen, I have created a relationship that is trustful,

1. While my matching percentage with Helen had been rated at 88 percent, Helen's match with me was rated as 99 percent.

loyal, and faithful, and those are necessary ingredients in any healthy and lasting relationship. We have both experienced disloyalty and unfaithfulness in the past, and we know we now share something profound and lasting. My hope for the future is to spend the rest of my life with Helen. She is my soul mate, and I would be lost without her. I may put up an independent front at times, but I would have a tough time without her.

10

Core Social Motives

Despite considerable progress in the field of personality theory, non-scientifically trained persons often jump to conclusions, judging personality as easy to assess and therefore routinely using it to explain or predict behavior. Scientifically trained persons might have a better handle, but personality theorists also disagree on how to measure personality, for from a scientific perspective, personality defies easy measurement. While to this point we have relied heavily on personality and spirituality models to contextualize Georgia, Helen, Jim, and Bob's life experiences, we need to enlarge our perspective to include what social psychologists call "situationism," thereby combining the joint power of personality *and* situations to explain and predict behavior.

Why does the social situation matter so much? Because human beings are social creatures, needing other people to survive and thrive. According to social psychologists, human behavior is strongly influenced by social acceptance, and humans respond to other people and seek social acceptance through five core social motives that help them survive and thrive individually and in groups: belonging, understanding, controlling, enhancing self, and trusting others.[1]

1. *Belonging*. Having close social ties is central to subjective well-being. Being ostracized threatens individual well-being, resulting in excessive stress and mood disorder. Problems in close relationships often disrupt hormonal balance, resulting in anxiety, depression, desperation,

1. Fiske, *Social Beings*, 12–21.

and futility, and contributing to poor physical health. Hence, social acceptability and belonging help people survive physically, emotionally, and spiritually.

2. *Understanding.* Since people are uncomfortable when surrounded by situations or circumstances they perceive as chaotic or incoherent, a fundamental motivation for behavior is making sense of one's environment. Shared understanding contributes to self-understanding, and both are necessary for individual and group survival. According to social psychologists, self-understanding and shared understanding help us make sense of ourselves and others, and help drive both attraction to similar others and prejudice against dissimilar others as well as certain kinds of social influence.
3. *Controlling.* The sense or degree of control people have in dealing with their social environment and themselves greatly influences the relationship between behavior and outcomes. People want to have some sense of control and competence, and a lack of control[2] contributes to a sense of helplessness. Research suggests that health and well-being accompany a sense of internal value and ability to influence others positively, and that people who feel they have internal control may be healthier, feel happier, and live longer than those who don't. Likewise, an imbalance between effort and reward or lack of control tends to result in poor mental and physical health. Needing control is the beginning of social effectiveness. A sense of control or effectiveness also encourages cooperative behavior in social settings, helping individuals fit into social groups and work cooperatively with others. If people know how to ask for help and then receive it, this also enhances social control and effectiveness.
4. *Self-enhancing.* This basic motive involves either maintaining self-esteem or being motivated by the possibility of self-improvement. When these are present, people feel good about themselves, accepting they are loveable and good. Conversely, those who feel terrible about themselves often lack the motivation to perform even the most basic tasks, such as getting out of bed in the morning, undertaking challenges, or meeting social obligations. Low self-esteem can result from

2. When I use the term "control," I do not mean to say that individuals should feel free to manipulate those in charge, but only that the opportunity exists to interact with those in authority.

neglect or rejection by important social others, leading such individuals to engage in socially and self-destructive behaviors such as substance abuse, irresponsible sexuality, aggression, and eating disorders. Likewise, when people feel good about themselves and others, they attempt to cooperate, thereby bonding with their social groups. In this regard, self-enhancement encourages personal growth and thus, self-improvement. Self-enhancement comprises both self-esteem and self-improvement.

5. *Trusting*. This basic motive involves seeing the world as a benevolent place. Thus, self-enhancement leads to group enhancement. While trusting makes us vulnerable, it also expects good outcomes, for when we are properly related to others, we tend to see the best not only in them, but also in ourselves. Trust facilitates daily life. It makes people both liked and likeable, and with good reason. Trusting people tend to be honest, generous, and compassionate. Distrusting people tend to be suspicious, vindictive, resentful, and isolated.

   Whereas trusting people naturally go with the flow, distrusting people search for nonobvious alternative explanations for other people's or other group's behavior, easily resorting to suspicious views such as conspiracy theories or solutions. A trusting orientation, compared with a paranoid or depressive orientation, facilitates people's interactions with others. Think how socially ineffective people are when they always expect the worst from other people. Trust is social glue. Trust facilitates group cohesion because it is both rewarding and efficient. Because trust promotes participation, it averts social harm. When people are suspicious of one another, society suffers, but when people trust others, group life works better.

   While trust is a form of social intelligence, it operates through emotional channels. While people's assumptions about the trustworthiness and benevolence of others make them optimistic about themselves, their families, and their marriages, when their world is devastated by trauma, especially trauma caused by other people, or when they are impacted by betrayal, exploitation, or hostility, they tend to be maladjusted, discouraging mutual helping and group loyalty.

As we contemplate these five core social motives, it is important to note that they take different forms in different cultures, be they familial, racial, economic, social, religious, or national in nature. For example, while North

American and European cultures are more individualist on the whole—meaning they emphasize the autonomous or self-sufficient person—Asian, African, South American, and native American cultures, both in their native settings or in dispersed settings, on average are more collectivist—meaning that they emphasize groups such as the family, the tribe, the clan, the community, the organization, and the country over the individual.

Similarly, even within the United States, although the predominant orientation is individualist, various regions differ in degree of individualism and collectivism. For example, collectivism is extremely high in Hawaii but also in California, Utah, the deep south, and among ethnic pockets in urban settings across the country. The most individualist regions by far are the Rocky Mountain and Great Plains areas, encompassing recent frontier and livestock-herding societies. In more individualist cultures, people put each person's own needs over the group, whereas in more collectivist cultures, people put group needs over individual needs.

Epigenetics, Brain Plasticity, and Behavior Modification

Locked inside the DNA of every human being is an endless story—about origins, ancestors, fate, and much more. Until recently, these secrets were inaccessible. However, with the help of new technologies, scientists are now reading the hidden DNA within all species, making remarkable discoveries about ourselves and our fellow species. In the years since the mid-nineteenth century, when Austrian monk Gregor Mendel pioneered the science of genetics, though the mid-twentieth century, when Francis Crick and James Watson deciphered the structure of the DNA molecule, to the mapping of all three billion base pairs of our DNA by the Human Genome Project, science has uncovered astonishing links between genetics and environment.

Epigenetics, the science of living DNA, charts the chemical pathways that spur DNA into action by turning genes on and off. This rapidly advancing discipline has overturned traditional ideas about heredity, revealing that both the environment and behavior—our own and that of our ancestors—affect how our genes work. Adding a new twist to the nature-versus-nurture debate, epigenetics researchers have discovered that:

- We inherit more than we suspect. Changes that affect our behavior, including trauma, mental disorders, dietary intake, and substance abuse, can be transmitted between generations.
- Behavior modification works quickly. Twenty minutes of exercise or just one meal can transform how our genes function.
- Environmental degradation can impair genetic machinery. Pollution from a wide range of chemicals has long-lasting effects on gene expression.
- Diet and lifestyle influence our behavior and self-image. Like these influences, aging is largely an epigenetic phenomenon, as is our susceptibility to many diseases, including our body's ability to fight infection.

As the science of epigenetics makes clear, our behavior as well as our social and natural environment can influence and even alter personality traits that were previously thought to be hardwired into our genetic code. Despite the prevailing Darwinian emphasis on natural selection and the survival of the fittest, could nineteenth-century French biologist Jean-Baptiste Lamarck have been right about the inheritance of acquired characteristics? While transgenerational epigenetic inheritance is difficult to prove, the flexibility of behavior is clearly supported by the plasticity of the brain.[3] As we now know, learning is a form of behavioral flexibility, a plasticity of mind. As the human brain develops, it wires itself as a function of the relevant genes. Likewise, as it learns, the brain is able to rewire itself as a function of the relevant environment. The brain constantly changes, and as plasticity of the brain is essential for behavioral change, so "our ability to modify our behavior is a function of the brain's ability to modify its own structure."[4]

While many might be surprised to learn that our external environment affects us through our genes by modulating their activity, neuroscientists are discovering that this influence does not affect our genes directly. Rather, environmental influences on our genes are mediated by changes in the cells in which our genes reside. Different kinds of cells respond differently to the same environmental factor, whether it is social stress or food deprivation in the womb. As such, and despite the fact that all of the cells in our body have the same genes, any environmental effect in us is cell type-specific. For example, our liver cells will react one way to poor nutrition, our neurons will react in a different way, and many cell types won't react

3. Plasticity is the brain's ability to learn or change with experience.

4. Steen, *Evolving Brain*, 163.

at all. Therefore, in determining environmental influence on gene action, scientists look at particular cell population, such as neurons in a particular part of the brain, liver cells, pancreatic cells, and so on.

This helps to explain why there can be dramatic examples of discordance in genetically identical twins. Nature's clones are far from identical, which is why the term "identical twins" has been replaced by monozygotic twins. While Georgia and Helen are identical in many ways, they are significantly different in other ways. While some of these discordances can be attributed to biochemical randomness, called mutation, others are likely epigenetic in nature. While some epigenetic variations occur randomly, most occur in response to our environment, such as the food we eat, the pollutants to which we are exposed, and even our social influences and interactions. Naturally, twins are less different epigenetically than non-twins, not only because they often share similar environments throughout their lives, but because of the environment they experienced in the womb. Whatever their mother's diet was during that period, it affected them equally. The same goes for whatever stress their mother experienced during pregnancy. More typical siblings, however, can experience quite different fetal environments. In such cases, the epigenetic alterations that result can make one or the other more susceptible to such things as obesity, diabetes, heart disease, and atherosclerosis, but also depression, anxiety, and schizophrenia.

Nevertheless, as we now know, twins can and will continue diverging epigenetically throughout the course of their lives, and these epigenetic differences can make one twin or the other more susceptive to ailments such as Alzheimer's disease, lupus, and cancer. The good news here is that unlike mutations, epigenetic changes are reversible. The goal of much medical epigenetics is to find ways to reverse pathological epigenetic events. Many see in epigenetics the potential for a medical revolution, even for what those in the spiritual realm might call "miracles."

Until recently, the idea that neurons in the mammalian brain could divide, or that neurons could be born in the adult brain, was considered a heresy. Since the 1980s, this dogma began to change, and it changed so rapidly and profoundly that no one now questions that new neural pathways develop well into adulthood. Though the vast majority of nerve cells or neurons in the human brain are formed by the time of birth, neural pathways in the brain can be created throughout the life of individuals, even during their old age. Practically speaking, this comes to mean that we are never too old to change our views, perspectives, behavior, lifestyle, and even our mental and physical health. While the brain has a limited capacity for regeneration, it is now possible "to teach an old dog new tricks."

What we are learning from epigenetics, brain plasticity, and behavior modification is evident not only in the life journeys of our four protagonists but in our own exodus stories as well. Substantial and ongoing cognitive, behavioral, and spiritual transformation is not only possible but probable for us all, for when God (or whatever we call our higher power) is active in our lives, all is possible.

Manna in the Wilderness

Like the Israelites in the wilderness, people called to the insecurities, uncertainties, and risks of the second half of life sometimes yearn to return to the past. Like the Israelites, we become nostalgic for "the good old days in Egypt, even though it had been filled with bitterness and enslavement: "We remember the fish we used to eat in Egypt for nothing, the cucumbers, the melons, the leeks, the onions, and the garlic, but now our strength is dried up, and there is nothing at all but the manna to look at" (Numb 11:5–6).

Sometimes the miracle of the manna that falls daily from heaven in the wilderness of life does not satisfy our hunger for certainty and security. Sometimes we miss the predictability and sense of control we felt growing up, where we felt in control.

Though in actuality the Israelites had been oppressed and enslaved by the Egyptians, the Israelites wandering in the wilderness looked back at their time in Egypt with nostalgia because they could not bear the uncertainty they faced as free people. Freedom is, ultimately, uncertain and unpredictable. One of the first lessons people of faith must learn in order to be free is how to trust in the unknown.

In the biblical account of the Exodus, manna was a vehicle for learning this lesson. While in the wilderness, Israelites would go out and gather their daily supply of manna—just enough for that day. The manna provided the necessary preparation for becoming a free people, for freedom requires an ability to bear uncertainty, to trust in the unfolding journey. The manna challenged the Israelites to see something new and fresh in their daily routine. Instead of seeking the answers that might put their questions to rest, the manna taught the Israelites to live the questions, to find the new in the old, and to keep moving forward, ever living with hope. When we see existence alive with possibility, we leave Egypt, our first half of life patterns of bondage and constriction, and cross our midlife Jordans into second half of life awareness.

Up to this point, our protagonists have been characters in a story. While their stories to this point have come to an end, they are now free to live their endings unhindered, unfettered, and unscripted. Their journeys, like all our exodus stories, continue, for this is not

THE END

Appendix

A Wedding Homily[1]

Friends and family: We gather here today to celebrate the great truth that no matter where we find ourselves, when two or more are gathered together in the name of all that is sacred and holy, there is love. And love is a profound mystery that two souls can reach across the great river that separates one solitary heart from another, and set out on a dangerous and thrilling journey where in an instant, in a miracle, two become one. Love is the ship we build with compassion, forgiveness, and faith to travel the river of life together. Love is the dance of life; it is the greatest of contracts; the sweetest of promises:

- To keep each other afloat amid the storms.
- To keep each other laughing amid the sorrow and faithful amid the darkness.
- To rejoice together in the morning.
- To honor each other in the evening.

Love is a gift from God—the source of this love and of the river itself; the one who carries us from one shore to the next.

And now I pronounce you lover and beloved. May God bless your marriage!

1. This homily is adapted from the Hallmark movie *Signed, Sealed, Delivered: To the Altar.*

Bibliography

Baldacci, David. *Wish You Well*. New York: Warner, 2000.

Bourgeault, Cynthia. *The Wisdom Jesus: Transforming Heart and Mind*. Boston: Shambhala, 2008.

Coan, Richard W. *Hero, Artist, Sage, or Saint? A Survey of Views on What Is Variously Called Mental Health, Normality, Maturity, Self-Actualization, and Human Fulfillment*. New York: Columbia University Press, 1977.

Davies, Oliver. *Meister Eckhart: Selected Writings*. New York: Penguin, 1994.

Fiske, Susan T. *Social Beings: Core Motives in Social Psychology*. 4th ed. Hoboken, NJ: Wiley, 2018.

Francis, Richard C. *Epigenetics: The Ultimate Mystery of Inheritance*. New York: Norton, 2011.

Gissis, Snait B., and Eva Jablonka. *Transformations of Lamarckism*. Cambridge, MA: The MIT Press, 2000.

Hesse, Hermann. *Demian: The Story of Emil Sinclair's Youth*. Translated by Michael Roloff and Michael Lebeck. New York: Harper & Row, 1965.

———. *Narcissus and Goldmund*. Translated by Ursule Molinaro. New York: Farrar, Straus & Giroux, 1968.

———. *Siddhartha: An Indian Poem*. Translated by Susan Bernofsky. New York: Modern Library, 2006.

———. *Steppenwolf*. Translated by Basil Creighton. New York: Holt, Rinehart and Winston, 1982.

Hollis, James. *Finding Meaning in the Second Half of Life: How to Finally, Really Grow Up*. New York: Gotham, 2006.

———. *The Middle Passage: From Misery to Meaning in Midlife*. Toronto: Inner City Books, 1993.

Homes, Urban T. *The History of Christian Spirituality*. New York: Seabury, 1980.

Jung, C. G. *Psychological Types: or, The Psychology of Individuation*. New York: Pantheon, 1962.

Myers, Isabel Briggs, with Peter B. Myers. *Gifts Differing: Understanding Personality Type*. Palo Alto, CA: Davies-Black, 1980.

O'Connor, Elizabeth. *Journey Inward, Journey Outward*. New York: Harper & Row, 1968.

Plotkin, Bill. *Nature and the Human Soul: Cultivating Wholeness and Community in a Fragmented World*. Novato, CA: New World Library, 2008.

———. *Soulcraft: Crossing into Mysteries of Nature and Psyche*. Novato, CA: New World Library, 2003.

Richardson, Peter Tufts. *Four Spiritualities*. Palo Alto, CA: Davies-Black, 1996.

Rohr, Richard. *Falling Upward: A Spirituality for the Two Halves of Life*. San Francisco: Jossey-Bass, 2011.

———. *The Universal Christ: How a Forgotten Reality Can Change Everything We See, Hope For, and Believe*. New York: Convergent, 2019.

Steen, R. Grant. *The Evolving Brain: The Known and the Unknown*. Amherst, NY: Prometheus, 2007.

Teresa of Ávila. *The Interior Castle*. Translated by Mirabai Starr. New York: Riverhead, 2004.

Vande Kappelle. Robert. *Dark Splendor: Spiritual Fitness for the Second Half of Life*. Eugene: OR: Resource, 2015.

———. *Outgrowing Cultic Christianity: Restoring the Role of Religion*. Eugene, OR: Wipf & Stock, 2021.

Westerhoff, John. *Spiritual Life: The Foundation for Preaching and Teaching*. Louisville: Westminster John Knox, 1994.

www.ingramcontent.com/pod-product-compliance
Lightning Source LLC
Chambersburg PA
CBHW060344100426
42812CB00003B/1119
* 9 7 8 1 6 6 6 7 8 2 8 0 6 *